Colors of Heaven

Beginnings Never End

Colors of Heaven: Beginnings Never End

Copyright © 2022 by Lynn Monet

Foreword

As a geriatrics and end of life care nurse, I have observed hundreds of people close to death, from months to minutes. I have been at the bedside of more than eighty people who have crossed over in my presence. The similarities in the transitioning into death, death itself and afterlife as the soul moves forward into what most call heaven or home is consistent. I have observed, not only from a professional medical standpoint, but also a spiritual and personal one.

A better understanding is needed about what really happens when someone passes away. I hope to bring comfort, support and understanding to those who need it, especially those who have lost a loved one or are diagnosed with a terminal illness. I hope to dispel the fearful stigma of dying and the finality of death and to bring enlightenment to the loved ones who are left behind. Our soul never dies. Death is like the shedding of one's skin.

From a very early age, I have had the ability to see inter-dimensionally. This means I see frequency many cannot. This is also referenced as second sight. My stories are shared within this book. I am not trying to force my findings on anyone. Take from this book what resonates with you.

This book is not based on religion. It simply just "Is". In all the deaths I have observed, and viewing the familiar preparations on the other side, I've learned the only thing that keeps a soul earthbound after the opportunity to cross over is themselves. Freedom of choice reigns whether one is alive or dead.

I stay in connection with my family on the other side – mother, father, sister, and brother, who have also taken a major part in this book. My youngest daughter designed the cover of the book with the knowledge of how it would look before she even started. She also added the "Beginnings Never End" into the title.

Contents

1.	Did You Know?	1
2.	Pact Making and Events	23
3.	Our Souls are Eternal! Our Physical Bodies are not!	30
4.	The Physical Phases of Dying	44
5.	Robin	76
6.	To Cross Over or Not to Cross Over	123
7.	Visitations	133
8.	What Happens After We Cross Over?	145
9.	Spirituality and Religion	152
10.	Our Thoughts	165
11.	Food for Thought	174
12.	From the Other Side	187
13.	End of Life Directives	200

Chapter 1

Did You Know?

Did you know that heaven smells different to each individual person? Usually, the scent is something one has enjoyed the smell of or found comforting here on earth. Did you know that even though souls do not eat food on the other side, all they have to do is think about a specific earthly food and the sensation and satisfying flavor of eating it comes to them? Wouldn't that have been a nice option to have on earth, eat all you want and not have to watch the calories?

Did you know that time on the other side gives them one day equivalent to approximately twenty of our earth years? They do not have seasons and the temperature is equivalent to mid-seventies in degrees Fahrenheit, with a consistent light breeze. If a spirit wants to enjoy the earthly seasons, they can just think of whichever season they want to enjoy and they go to it instantly – usually to a place on a planet with season changes.

There is no light source such as the sun. The light illuminates from within the atmosphere itself. Its lighting is similar to when a person is standing under a tree in the shade looking into the light without glare. Everything is alive, every flower and blade of grass. When one observes these living things, one connects to them and feels its light and life pulsating within.

Did you know they are able to be fully present in six places simultaneously? This means they can be riding with you in your car to work – which they often do – and also be fully present at a relative's house sitting at the breakfast table.

Did you know they keep all of their senses after crossing over? Plus, a few abilities are added, one being telepathy. Did you know, they do have individual homes there? They have similar furniture similar to ours, only much grander.

Oftentimes when we are attracted to artwork on this earthly third dimensional plane, (or in the case of an artist, artwork that we paint), the artwork are replicas of those we have in our homes on the other side. If one speaks to an artist about their process, they often will tell you that they already have a picture in their minds of how a portrait will look when completed. This is why. Unbeknownst to them in this lifetime, they have not only seen the image before, but they have already created it before, as well.

Did you know your loved ones have met and embraced your children waiting to come in and who are born after the soul's crossing over? Sometimes a person near death will talk about children who have not been born yet.

Sara

I remember being in the room with Sara. Her aunt, Janet, was my client, who was in the last stages of cancer. Janet had started to transition.

"When are you going to have those beautiful baby girls?" I overheard Janet ask Sara.

She went on to describe the baby girls in great detail.

"The two girls look the exact same and both look just like Sara," she said. "They have blond curls and dimples with big, brown eyes."

"I wish that could be!" Sara replied sadly.

Sara reminded her aunt that she was unable to have children.

"Greg and I have been trying for twenty-five years with no results. I feel now, at forty-five years of age, I'm too old," Sara said. "I'm just starting menopause. My doctor even recently recommended a hysterectomy."

Yet Janet looked at Sara and insisted, "These are your children!

"You better have those babies soon! I want to see them before I go home to Jesus!"

Janet, in her last days, was transitioning in and out, testing the dimensions. This appears to embodied souls as being in and out of sleep and consciousness. A day passed and Janet had not opened her eyes or said anything for about twenty-four hours.

Sara, who had been staying in the room with Janet, was leaving to meet family at the airport while the hospice nurse stayed behind with Janet. Sara kissed Janet and told her she would be back in an hour with Uncle Charles, who was Janet's youngest brother.

When Sara and her Uncle Charles arrived back to the facility, they stopped at the nurse's station and I walked with them down to Janet's room. When we neared the door, we could overhear Janet chattering away.

"She woke up about fifteen minutes after you left," the hospice nurse told Sara and Charles. "The first thing Janet said was, 'Where are those babies?' I told her, 'I don't know about any babies.' She kept saying, 'Sara's babies!'"

Sara told the nurse Janet had been talking about two little girls that she thought were Sara's.

"I don't have any children."

Just then, Janet piped up and insisted, "Sara, I saw you! You were holding them, one in each arm. They were so beautiful!"

Janet closed her eyes for the last time about two hours later. She transitioned through the veil into the other side the next day.

About six months later, I saw Sara coming on to the unit to visit another client.

She had a nice round, protruding belly.

I had to ask, and she told me the story. Several weeks after Janet's crossing over, Sara and her husband started looking for children to adopt, when all of a sudden, Sara became ill.

"I went to my doctor thinking I had mononucleosis," she said. "I was exhausted and could not eat from the nausea. The doctor ran some tests and all that came back pretty normal."

Then the doctor asked when Sara had her last menstrual cycle.

"I am in menopause," Sara responded. "My menstrual cycle has been irregular for a year now. The last menstruation I had was about three months ago."

The doctor recommended a pregnancy test.

Sara laughed and said, "There is no way I am pregnant!" But she reluctantly agreed.

The urine test came back – Sara was pregnant.

"The doctor was concerned about the size of my uterus in relation to the tentative due date," Sara said. "He said, 'Your uterus is abnormally enlarged in comparison to what it should be. Either you are farther along or have more than one baby in there.' He asked if I could come back the next morning to have an ultrasound done in the office to determine with more certainty how far along I was.

"I went home in shock. I told my husband, Greg, that I had a test to be done in the doctor's office the next morning but did not tell him why. I just told him I needed a ride home and would not be able to drive after the test."

The next morning, they pulled up into the doctor's parking lot. Sara was taken back to the exam room as her husband sat in the waiting area.

A few minutes later, the ultrasound technician opened the door to the waiting area and asked Greg to come in. Greg got up and came into the hallway, concerned, and asked if everything was alright. The technician nodded yes. Greg entered the room.

Sara was lying on the exam table.

"Sit down," she said, "there's some big news."

Perplexed, Greg complied.

Sara asked the technician to turn the screen so that Greg could also see. Greg clutched Sara's hand, braced for the possibility of bad news.

Sara beamed at Greg. "I want you to meet our children."

It turned out that Sara, unbeknownst to her, was pregnant with identical twins. Sara was in the early stages of pregnancy before her aunt crossed over. She just hadn't known it.

Greg, with tears running down his face, stated proudly, "I'm going to be a dad!"

He then asked the technician, "Are they healthy? We are older folks you know."

"The doctor will read the final report," the technician replied, "but I do not think you have anything to worry about."

Later, during an amniocentesis, they found they were having healthy identical girls.

I got to see Sara a few times more as she visited several clients from time to time on my unit. Her daughters were blonde with brown eyes and dimples. They grew up more and more to look like their mom, just like I remembered Janet had said they would.

Mary

Mary was forty-nine and had never been married, nor was she dating anyone. She lived alone and liked it that way. She was also an only child.

Her mother had been placed with hospice on my unit. I was in the room during one of Mary's visits with her mother, Beverly. Beverly had started to talk about seeing loved ones in her room.

"There is a little boy here and he is calling me Grandma," Beverly said to Mary.

"I don't have any children," Mary replied matter-of-factly. "And I am an only child. Plus I am in menopause, so I cannot imagine why a child would be calling you 'Grandma'!"

"He says he is your boy," Beverly insisted, "and he continues to call me Grandma."

Mary looked up at me, twirling her finger around her ear in a "she is crazy" motion. "I feel like my mother is hallucinating."

Over a period of days, Beverly declined until she was no longer responsive.

Mary stopped in the hallway to let me know she was stepping away to go the breakroom where they had vending machines to get something to eat. When Mary returned, she was smiling.

"I just ran into a very nice man who helped me with change in the break room," she said. "He just lost his wife."

They struck up a conversation while he was waiting for additional family to arrive.

"We exchanged phone numbers," Mary said, "just to give each other support through our time of grief."

Mary's mother, Beverly, ended up crossing over later that day.

I ran into Mary in a grocery store about four years later. She had a toddler riding in her cart. She shared with me that after meeting the gentlemen in the breakroom, the two spoke a couple times a week over the phone. Their conversations were totally platonic for about a year when Steve decided to ask Mary out. Mary reluctantly said yes.

They went out and had the best time and were married six months later. Shortly after, Mary, who was approaching age fifty-one at the time, was feeling tired often and found that certain smells of familiar things made her nauseated.

She went to her doctor to find out why she was not feeling well (and had not been for weeks). The doctor drew her blood and sent it off to the lab. He also did a pap-smear since she was due for one. He noticed her uterus felt enlarged. His immediate concerns were cancer, so he asked her to return three days later for a sonogram of her pelvis.

Mary returned to the doctor's office for her appointment. She was prepped for an ultrasound. In the meantime, Mary's blood work came back.

The results indicated a pregnancy.

The technician began the ultrasound and started taking measurements of the "mass" on the screen. The doctor peeked into the room.

Mary asked in a concerned tone, "What is the mass on the screen?"

"That's your baby," her doctor replied. "I suggest you get on pre-natal vitamins and see your obstetrician."

Mary was in shock and now had a lot of questions, as she joyously heard her baby's heartbeat. Mary had completed her first trimester and was about two weeks into her second trimester. She also found out that it was a boy that day!

She then went on to share how she told her husband.

"I wrapped up a blue onesie with a bib that said, "Daddy's Little Helper" and wrote the due date on the small blue baby socks in a gift box. He opens it and asks, 'Who's pregnant?' I blurted out, 'We are!' And he says jokingly, 'Well, there goes the boat!'

"He also said it would be worth it to finally have a son," Mary said. "He has four grown daughters; this is his first son. He was excited."

Did you know our deceased loved ones often show themselves in family pictures? Look in between or off to the sides of the embodied people in the photograph. Also look for a bubble-like orb. Spirits can be seen by people preparing to depart and younger children who have recently arrived. We all are born with these abilities to connect with spirits. However, the nurturing of these gifts are required to make it grow and the lack of nurturing to go dormant. Younger children have no discerning filters; the filters form as they mature. The filters efface when a person is closer to crossing over. The thinner filters allow the embodied souls to see and hear bodiless souls.

Abigail

Abigail and her husband came to the upscale facility I was working in as a nurse. They needed all levels of care, especially for Abigail's husband, whose health was declining.

Shortly after they moved in, Abigail slipped and fell, fracturing her hip. She was placed on my unit while recovering from her surgery. Abigail was a vivacious and elegant lady. She never had any children and most of her family was either deceased or lived in a different state.

Abigail enjoyed our visits whenever I worked. We built a professional yet comfortable rapport.

One day I arrived on shift and started my medication pass, which led me into Abigail's room. Abigail had a very concerned look on her face.

"Lynn, do you think I am crazy?" she blurted.

I winked teasingly and cocked my head to the side. "What do you mean by 'crazy'?"

"I mean like, 'crazy' crazy," Abigail replied.

"No," I said, "why?"

"I see my parents," Abigail said, "and I know they died twenty plus years ago, but they come to visit me.

"I like seeing my parents; it makes me happy," she continued, "but the doctors and staff claim that I am hallucinating and are planning to start me on medication for hallucinations tomorrow morning."

Tearfully, Abigail asked, "Lynn, do you think I am seeing hallucinations?"

"Do *you* think you are seeing hallucinations?" I asked her.

"No."

"Well then, I don't think you are, either." As I said it, I was thinking about how I have a different belief system in comparison to most people.

Abigail continued to express her concerns about the new medication orders. I reassured her that I had been told at shift change that she had been cleared to return to her apartment the next day, and as her advocate, she had the right to refuse any medication she does not want. Abigail was pleased to be going home.

About six months later, Abigail's health started to decline, and once again she was placed on my unit. Now Abigail was not only talking about her deceased parents, but also about a woman and little girl who had been coming to visit her. This created a bit of a problem for the facility, as Abigail was sneaking cookies and desserts out of the dining room into her room to give to the little girl. This was drawing ants to Abigail's room. The staff had to start checking her for hidden food before leaving the dining room.

Abigail had more medications for hallucinations added, yet she continued to talk about the visits from spirits.

One day, I had volunteered to cover a day shift for a friend of mine. I normally worked nights.

After lunchtime, the residents were settled back into their rooms, and I headed down the hallway to start my treatments. As I passed Abigail's room on my left, I noticed Abigail sitting in her recliner next to a large window with an air conditioner underneath. She was leaning forward with a piece of yellow wrapped butterscotch candy, holding it out as if offering it to someone. It would have appeared to anyone else passing by that she was talking to and trying to feed the candy to her air conditioner.

As I passed, I noticed a young woman. She had long, waist length black hair, and wore a denim ankle length skirt and white peasant style blouse. She appeared Hispanic or Native Indian. In front of the woman stood a little girl who also had long black hair, only with bangs. She wore a light-colored dress with a pinafore and black Mary Jane style shoes that were very cute. They were both facing Abigail and standing in front of her. Abigail was offering the candy to the little girl.

"Abigail's got visitors today," I thought happily.

I continued a few more steps and it came to mind that I had not remembered seeing the lady with the little girl signing in at the nurse's desk. I stopped and remembered that it was a regulation to have a head count of souls in the building just in case of an emergency and needing to evacuate.

So I turned around and walked the few steps back to Abigail's room. I knocked on the door frame, as her door was already open, and got permission to enter.

When I walked past the bathroom into Abigail's room, there was nobody there except for Abigail, who was still leaning forward with the candy in her hand offering it to the now invisible little girl. I could see waffling to the air and knew the spirits were still in the room.

"I want you to meet my friends," Abigail piped up. "Isn't the little girl beautiful?"

"Yes, she is," I replied.

Abigail's eyes got big as she sat back in her chair, then leaned forward again with a purpose.

"Can you see them?"

And I said, "Yes."

Abigail's eyes got squinty, and she said in a loud whisper, "Don't tell anybody that you can see them! They will put you on medication and call you nuts!"

I couldn't help myself and chuckled. "Our secret is safe with me. I'm glad you have friends visiting today."

I remember thinking how amazing it was that despite the fact that she was on lots of medication for hallucinations, she was still seeing spirits, because they were not hallucinations.

I started to leave the room. I acknowledged the spirits and asked Abigail if I could pull her door shut so that she could enjoy the visit with her friends in private. Abigail agreed and thanked me. I reminded her to use the nurse call light when she was finished, and I would come back and open the door if she wanted.

About a month later, Abigail's health started to decline rapidly. I came on my night shift and entered Abigail's room. She appeared to be sleeping. I stroked her forearm and hand and softly said, "Miss Abigail, it's Lynn, and I am here to check your blood pressure."

Abigail's eyes opened and she smiled. "I'm so glad I get to see you one more time. My parents are coming to take me home tomorrow and I wanted to thank you for all you have done for me."

"It was my pleasure," I said. "I hope your transition home goes well."

"And you are very much loved on the other side!" Abigail said. "They want you to keep doing what it is that you have been doing."

My eyes welled up with tears. I kissed her cheek and gave her a hug. I told her that we would meet again someday

"Oh yes, we will!" Abigail responded excitedly.

That night I made rounds on Abigail throughout the night, and she was no longer responsive. I was off the next day when Abigail followed her parents home at around 10:30 pm. At around that time, I was thinking of Abigail, and I could feel her saying, "I made it home!"

In my experience, there are three types of deaths: a natural death, a sudden death and a near-death experience. Each category is received differently on the other side, yet similarly within its own category. I will go into each topic much deeper in upcoming chapters.

When dying is a natural decline, which most deaths are, a person starts to transition. As they get closer to their time of crossing over, filters between dimensions start to efface. Their embodied soul exits and reenters their body during this time. This is referred to by end of life care professionals as "rallying." This gives the embodied soul the opportunity to reconnect with loved ones on the other side and "test the waters" so to speak.

Embodied onlookers will notice times where the body of their loved one is breathing, but their feet are flaccid and their eyes are glazed over. They are nearly impossible to rouse. I call this the "lights are on but no one's home" stage. When the spirit returns to the body, the eyes brighten and the feet and toes perk into a more normal upright position. When the soul returns to their earthly body, onlookers often overhear their transitioning loved one mention or even talk directly to deceased souls that only they can see. This in and out process can go on for days.

Edna

Edna was a client that was only on my unit for three weeks. She was totally blind and had lost her vision ten years before. She was in an active decline.

I was at the nurse's station when Edna's son and daughter approached the desk. They told me that Edna was talking to people in the room that were not there.

"I will walk with you back to Edna's room," I told them, "to see if there is anything I can do to make her more comfortable."

Upon entering Edna's room, Edna was smiling and reaching up into the air, grasping gently, as if someone was handing her something very delicate.

"Edna, who are you talking to?" I asked.

"George," she answered.

Her daughter's skin blanched and she had to sit down.

"George is my father!" Edna's daughter said. "He died about nine years ago."

"And he is glad you are taking good care of Pixie," Edna chimed in.

"I have Pixie," said Edna's son. "Pixie was my parents' poodle. When my father died, because Mom was blind, I had to take her. She is still alive and about fourteen years old."

He looked at me. "Do you think Mom is hallucinating?"

"Do *you* think your mother is hallucinating?" I asked.

He hesitated. "I don't know, but this is kind of freaky."

"Could I try something?" I asked. "In my experience, this is normal behavior, as loved ones do come in to gather their loved ones at the time of death."

I asked Edna if I could ask George a question and she nodded 'yes.'

I asked George out loud, "What color shirt does your son have on?"

Through Edna, George responded, and Edna said, "Yellow."

"Hi, Dad," said Edna's son. He realized in that moment his mom was not hallucinating; she was actually seeing loved ones that both he and his sister knew.

Did you know deceased loved ones can move light weight objects like feathers, hairs, cards, and pictures? They can make lights flicker and children's toys turn on and off when no one is near them. When asking them to do something more physical, keep in mind that their time frame is different than ours and it may not be an immediate response – although it could be. Please avoid Ouija boards for communication. They open portals and often allow unwanted darker entities to enter our dimension. Once they do, they won't leave.

Did you know your pets and younger children can see spirits who have crossed over, as well as ghosts who have not? Speaking of pets, did you know that your pets cross over, too, and will greet you after the initial homecoming? They come in the second phase. All of your pets, even the ones you don't remember, and are reminded of when you cross over, will be there. Perhaps you had an elephant as a pet, at another time. It will be happy to see you.

Did you know your loved ones on the other side can help find your keys and other items that have been misplaced? They like being called on to help, but they will only help when called upon. This part is important to remember. Souls on the other side cannot interfere with one's freedom of choice. Therefore, they need to be asked for assistance. They will not give you the winning lotto numbers. Winning the lotto may not be part of your path in this life, so don't ask. If you are intended to be a lotto winner in this life, you will eventually know it when you win.

Did you know that the soul never dies? Did you know that your loved ones who have crossed over can hear every word you say out loud, especially when directed to them? They can also hear your thoughts, since that is how they communicate amongst themselves on the other side. They communicate telepathically and move about the dimensions through thought, as well.

They have a good sense of humor, too. This is fortunate for those who use profanity frequently and without thinking. If your time comes to cross over, and the first time you see an eight-foot-tall angel or other heavenly type being standing in front of you, you think, "Holy shit?" don't think you are hiding it just because you have not spoken it verbally. What you are thinking, you are saying over there. It might be a good idea now to start speaking and thinking in a more respectful and loving way, so as not to embarrass yourself later on.

One must be responsible for their thoughts, with or without a body. When in body, one manifests through their thoughts and outward verbalizations. In spirit, one's thoughts are as if they are on a party line. I will talk more about this in a later chapter.

Did you know the median age on the other side is thirty-five years old? Even babies are old souls.

Mrs. Little

Mrs. Little had been a resident in the skilled unit for three years. She had not spoken a single word that entire time. Her facial expression was flat and rarely changed. She had advanced Alzheimer's.

Mrs. Little had wheeled herself by foot down to the nurse's station and sat there. I was sitting at the nurse's desk.

"Hello, Mrs. Little," I said.

As usual, she said nothing.

In the hallway straight ahead of Mrs. Little, a member was actively passing. She was in the last stages of transitioning. Normally Mrs. Little would pass right by the room on her journey down the hall. Today, however, something seemed to hold her attention.

Mrs. Little appeared to be fixated on the hallway, particularly the first door on the right.

I stepped away from the desk into the charting room. Suddenly I heard a woman's voice saying, "Hey!"

Then, louder, a second time: "Hey!"

The tone sounded urgent.

I re-entered the nurse's station and looked to see who was calling out. There was no one other than Mrs. Little. I entered the hallway and looked both ways to see if someone needed assistance further down the hallway. I didn't see anyone.

I went back to the station and sat down. Mrs. Little opened her mouth and yelled, "Take me home!

"Please, please, take me home!"

I was shocked.

I immediately went to Mrs. Little's side. She continued to look down the hallway calling out, "Please! Please! I want to go home! Take me home!"

"Who are you talking to?" I asked.

"Look right there," she replied. She pointed into the hallway towards the declining member's room.

"Look at the angels," she said, excitedly. "Aren't they beautiful?"

Then she continued to yell into the hallway, "Please take me home!" over and over.

I looked down the hallway. At first I saw nothing. Then I looked harder and could see the misted veil with movement on the other side. I could see lots of people's spirits, angels, and large luminous beings, almost as if they were standing on stair steps or bleachers. There were so many that they were bulging out of the transitioning member's room into the hallway through the wall.

I replied to Mrs. Little, "Yes, they are magnificent."

Mrs. Littles eyes filled with tears of joy as she smiled from ear to ear, and she continued to call out.

The transitioning client passed away an hour later. The mist cleared away and the spirit beings left. Mrs. Little remained sitting still, looking down the hall, and once again became silent, never to speak a word again.

In the coming weeks, whenever I would mention to Mrs. Little about the angels we both saw in the hallway that day, her eyes sparkled in response. Mrs. Little passed away three months later in her sleep. Her room was filled with angels and loved ones from the other side at the time of her last breath.

Did you know souls can choose to cross over or remain earthbound at the time of death? Did you know our soul never dies? We simply shed our physical bodies.

Chapter 2

Pact Making and Events

Souls on the other side present themselves to other souls as their earthly identities. They are usually wearing robes or Grecian-style wrapped garments. The exception is when they are collecting a loved one who is transitioning over. They will then show up fully dressed in clothes they had worn in life – usually the ones they were buried in or the outfit their loved one last saw the soul in prior to death. They are aware that if the welcoming party of deceased relatives were to show up not dressed, it would be shocking to the transitioning soul. (I have only ever seen one naked male ghost and that is a story in another book.)

Their age appearance is one that the transitioning soul would recognize. For example, ninety-year-old grandma will look like ninety-year-old grandma to her grandchildren when it comes time for them to cross over.

Souls also often present with a fragrance that one might remember. Pleasant smell or unpleasant – like cigar smoke or a wound – the scent is recognizable but not offensive.

If you are comfortable talking about death, make a pact with your loved one prior to their death. This will make their earthly visits after crossing over more obvious.

Phyllis (My Mom)

When my mom, Phyllis, was declining from cancer and opted to no longer have treatments, she wanted to share her secret recipes with my family. These were unique foods she would prepare, especially during the holidays. Everyone loved her food.

She had the recipes in her head. She and I sat together and wrote them down. We figured out exactly what a pinch or dash measurement would be so as to get the taste as close to Phyllis's recipe as possible. Phyllis was also able to share the secrets and quirks of the preparation, so that her foods could continue to be served as a tradition at the family's holiday.

We went through family pictures. Phyllis divided up the photos she had collected over the years of her children, and the memorabilia, such as school awards and "I love you, Mommy" notes given by each child. She made a picture pouch for each one.

Phyllis was able to tell me who some of the relatives in older pictures were that I did not know or recognize. I wrote the names on the back of the photos and how they were related, so that they would be passed on to future generations.

I took Mom to visit her friends, family and places she enjoyed going. We had lasagna at her favorite restaurant weekly.

Phyllis was able to go through her things and give them directly to each person she wanted to have them.

Something Phyllis had always wanted to do was go camping. The opportunity arose when my brother came to visit our mom in his RV. I found a tent pad right across from where my brother was settled and set up camp in a tent. Mom was thrilled. We sang around a campfire while roasting marshmallows.

I took her for her first pedicure and manicure. She had no idea how nice pedicures were and instantly became addicted. I continue to take her to them until her death.

As the time drew closer for Mom to cross over, she and I made a pact. I asked her to confirm her visits from the other side by leaving one of her hairs behind. My mother had long, wavy white pearlescent hair that was unique to all the brunettes in our family.

On the day of Phyllis's funeral, I drew a bath with some bubbles at my house. While the tub was filling, I went to gather my clothes for the funeral. When I returned to the bathroom, lying straight, full length on top of the bubbles was a long, pearlescent white hair, as if it had been gently placed. I could feel my mother's smile, which in turn made me smile, too. I felt comforted.

I continued to find Phyllis's hairs frequently, even after I had moved into a new place and gotten a new car – both of which my mother had never been in.

Two years later, I was taking nursing classes at the university. I was stressing over taking an upcoming test that day in an extremely hard class. On the way to school, I stopped at the school bookstore to buy a three-ring binder and loose-leaf book for my class. After purchasing the items needed, I went straight from the bookstore to my car, then to the campus and classroom.

When I sat down at my desk, I took my newly purchased items out of the bag. I unwrapped the loose-leaf book and then opened the three-ring binder to put the loose-leaf pages inside. To my surprise, in the middle ring of the three-ring binder, was a long, white pearlescent hair looped in the teeth of the middle ring. It had been looped multiple times, appearing almost like a flower.

I knew there was no way that hair could have gotten there by itself. I knew it was from my mother and that my mom was near that day, cheering me on.

Phyllis continued, even after I moved twice, to leave her hairs purposely placed. With each hair, I know my mom has stopped by to check in, and this is a huge comfort to me.

Pacts can also be entered into after one has crossed over. Ask your loved one to send in a specific symbol of their presence. Pick something like turtles, lady bugs, or a song, and know that in that moment, they are with you.

Events

One's deceased family and friends are rejoicing right along with others at weddings, birthday parties and graduations, as well as other events one would want to have them attend, if they were still embodied. Often a person will hear another say how they wish some deceased person or people were also there to see an event. They are! They are aware of the event before you even know about it and prepare accordingly to be a part of it. They rejoice right along with you. If only one could hear the sounds of the rejoicing, one would be blown away by the beauty and be drawn in by the elation of it.

They keep their attendance of such events on what I call the "high, high" (not "down low," but meaning the same thing). Because their presence being known would take away from the greatness of the life event for the embodied soul. It would be very distracting. They fill bleacher-type seating in corners and near ceilings. They may even sit right next to you if there is a seat open. They usually do not sit on top of an embodied person or double occupy a seat, though. They like their own. Keep in mind, this is a little different with souls who have not crossed over and are still earthbound.

Just so you know, they have a form of coupling that, when performed, creates a continuous orgasmic, rapturous, bond between two souls. This orgasmic bond is continuous for as long as they are enmeshed in the act. They use this act for pleasure only. It is a combining of individual frequencies that are merged together as one. When this happens, the pairing resonate a unique sound together. This sound is only heard during the act. It is performed in the purest act of love and spirituality. It is something beyond sexuality as we know it here on the third dimension. There is a holiness and divinity to it that cannot be described well enough in human words. The energetic fusing that takes place is too intense for the human body to withstand more than a few seconds and is why embodied orgasms are cut short.

Sex

Sex here on earth is also a sacred act. The sexual act is to exchange the purest form of love between two people who are in love. The loving connection is also energetic and builds stronger over time. This is when two people are exclusively connected and monogamous. The energy layers with each contact bond them together. This bonding and monogamy protect them from outside sexually transmitted disease on a physical level, while spiritually it negates abruptions in one's spiritual field.

Each person filtering the other's essence when love is involved equally can be the most satisfying. Each leaves the other with an energetic gift. This is as close as embodied souls can come to the enmeshment felt in the fifth dimension.

The parties involved filter this loving energy back and forth between each other during the act of sex and while sleeping near each other. Their vibrations resonate harmoniously, and they become one.

However, this energetic rhythm can be negated, leaving one or both parties feeling unfulfilled. Recreational drugs are blockers of energy and intimacy. So is purposely inflicted pain. The loving act of sex was never meant to be performed with distorted minds. When the act is performed in an unloving way or by people not in love, it becomes a more darkened act of selfish gratification.

Whenever a person has sex with another, not only do their energies exchange, but any negative emotions and thoughts either carry are passed on to the other subconsciously, leaving them with feelings of the slag remaining.

When sex is unbalanced or shared with multiple partners, the energy flow is interrupted and never has the opportunity to connect in the way that it can become cyclical. It therefore always leaves one (usually the female more so than the male) or both of the people feeling empty after an intimate encounter, and unfulfilled shortly after the act is finished. Often people are oblivious to the abruption this unloving act causes in the energetic field around them.

The emptiness causes them to continue to seek more encounters, looking for the one who will finally fill the void. Earthy souls search for the heavenly connectedness in a partnership. However, if they keep having sex with strangers or people they do not have a love connection with, they will never have what they are seeking the most out of earthly sex: the spiritual connection part of it.

Chapter 3

Our Souls are Eternal! Our Physical Bodies are not!

Souls come and go – lives begin and end – like cars speeding on the Interstate with no exits. There are many definitions for the word 'die.' The definition used in this chapter is the passage from our physical life, leaving behind one's physical attributes and abilities. It is a shedding of our skin/body. Our bodies are the vessels that our souls use to be able to function on earth and be earthbound. They are temporary and wear out.

However, the soul itself lives on. The soul never dies! Therefore, your loved one is not really dead. They are very much alive and well. And the goodbye said at the bedside of a transitioning soul is not your last time to see them. You will meet again in another time and place in the not too far future.

Each person on this earth has their own definitions of what it means to both live and die, especially as they approach their time to cross over.

Greta

As her time to cross over approached, Greta worried that when she crossed over, her family would not recognize her. Particularly, she worried that her late husband, who died in his middle thirties, and her now in her nineties, would be turned off by her aged appearance.

Since our loved ones on the other side are checking in with us throughout our lives, they are aware of our aging process and when we cross over. When people cross over, they look the same to those on the other side as they did the last time those on the other side saw them before *they* crossed over. Once settled in, everyone's appearance age on the other side is thirty-five years of earth years. It is considered the perfect age in our life span and is the age before our earthly bodies begin to decline with age.

Most living things know when their time to cross over is drawing near, especially in the case of natural death. Even animals will sometimes wander off or look for a place to hide as they get closer to their time. There is a difference between a natural death, a sudden death and near-death experience.

The way each person views death is also unique to them. Death is much harder for the loved ones left behind than it is for the one leaving. Children are less afraid of the concept of death than adults. Nature versus nurture – death is a nature, and fear of anything, nurture. Fear of death is a learned behavior. Some people like to be alone when death happens, and others do not. Some people reference the cessation of life as their ascension or rebirth, and not death.

Unfortunately, most do not see dying in a positive way. However, rebirth and ascension is exactly what death is.

Phyllis (My Mom)

The day before my mother passed away naturally, she went around the facility she was in and told everyone goodbye. She even went so far as to tell one lady whose dog had died two days before that she would watch out and care for the dog until the owner herself crossed over. She told people she was going home the next day and requested to be moved to hospice where there was a bed waiting for her arrival.

Our family was notified of her transfer to hospice. My brother and I arranged to travel there as quickly as we could. I arrived first, with my son, Austin. Mom was resting and testing the dimensions as she went in and out. In many cases, loved ones leave the bodily vessel even before it stops breathing.

In my mother's case, she chose to stay in body right up until the end. Arriving at her bedside, I kissed her cheek and let her know we were there. Mom could hardly speak as she reached for my hand and held it to her heart.

"Love, love," she said, as she patted my hand gently against her chest. "I didn't think you were going to make it in time."

She saw Austin and said, "Awe, my Austin came, too," and those were the last words she spoke.

She had lost her swallowing reflex and was no longer able to verbally respond, but she still acknowledged us with mouth movements and raising her eyebrows up and down. People would stop by the room and say hello and Phyllis would respond facially. Her expressions were deliberate and appropriate.

After staying at her bedside, tending her for many hours, I had to take my son home. I kissed my mother and reassured her that I would be back in the morning. Her eyebrows went up and down in acknowledgment.

"Please keep her mouth moist and anything else she needs for comfort," I told the nurses. "And please call me if her time to pass is close."

I wanted to be with her during that time.

Her vital signs were still relatively stable despite her temperature being elevated. The feeling in her room was peaceful. I did not sense any spiritual activity at that time near her.

I made the hour drive home, slept two hours, and made plans with a friend to drop my youngest child off at school. Then I returned to my mother's bedside early the next morning.

I had only been gone from my mother's side a total of five hours. She was no longer able to open her eyes but would acknowledge with her eyebrows and attempts to mouth words with no sound. My mother was always very beautiful and remained that way on this last morning of her life. I took a warm washcloth and wiped off her face, neck, and hands. I applied her lipstick and combed her hair. I knew that her time was close. I kissed her and told her how much I loved her and that everyone here would be okay. It was okay for her to go home.

An hour passed and a visitor stopped by to see Mom. She talked about how much everyone loved my mom. A little while later, the minister stopped by and said a prayer.

It was about 12:00 pm. I was alone in the room with my mom, and I started to notice a misting on the other side of the room, directly across from me. As the mist grew thicker, I could see rippling within it, like a curtain or a veil.

As I watched the veil, I noticed here and there a hand, shoes, or shoulder temporarily peeking through, or someone walking past. The movement beyond the veil seemed very busy and excited. There seemed to be quite a bit, with many beings.

The movement behind the veil increased, and a feeling of joy and love began to emanate from the mist. The love emitting from the other side was encompassing and comforting. I was mesmerized.

The veil now extended the length of the room, like a wall. As the mist settled, the inter-dimensional veil started to efface next to my mother's right side, near her shoulder. An arch opened, large enough for a person to come through. The souls on the other side were waiting to bring my mother home.

The first soul to enter through the opening in the thinning veil was my mother's mother, who the family called "Gramma Girl." My deceased grandmother looked the same as she did the last time I had seen her. She even wore her two-piece pants suit she had made herself.

Gramma Girl walked over to my mother's bedside on her right side, opposite of me, and started to gently stroke my mother's forearm. My grandmother leaned forward, close up to my mother's right ear. She whispered something in my mother's ear then stood back up while continuing to stroke my mother's arm. My mother in turn responded to her mother by mouthing words and moving her eyebrows appropriately.

My gramma leaned forward and whispered into my mother's ear two more times that I noticed, before being distracted.

From behind my grandmother, I saw a gleefully waving hand. I looked at the hand and the beautiful face of my youngest sister, grinning from ear-to-ear, entered the room. She knew I could see her and was trying to get my attention.

Once we made eye contact, my sister ran around the back of the crowd of souls there. The veil had effaced even more, exposing more souls waiting. My sister hugged me. I could smell her perfume and feel her long dark hair falling over my face as she bent to embrace me. Her cheek rested on the top of my head, her hair a curtain around my face.

My eyes started to well up with tears again. I was so happy to see my beautiful sister Robin. I was also thankful that my sister would get to be with our mom now.

As my sister went back into the crowd, I noticed that the veil was gone. It was like the two dimensions had become one. I could see the people standing on the inside of heaven. There must have been eighty or more people smiling and joyfully waiting for my mother's return home. They had all prepared a glorious reception just for my mother's arrival. Some of the spirits I recognized and some I did not.

I was surprised to see my ex-husband's deceased parents standing together to the left, away from the crowd in front. They were very good people and I loved them. They knew it. In that moment, even though I was in a nasty divorce from their son, they were there. I felt their condolences and that, regardless of their grown children's adverse feelings towards me, they both wanted me to know that they cared about me and my mother. They had separated themselves from the crowd to make sure I saw them, and for me to know that they were there. It was a comfort to me. I appreciated their kind gesture.

I spoke out loud to my mother. "Gramma Girl and Robin are here!" I told her again that I loved her, and to give Robin and Gramma a big hug from me.

Then I said, "It's time to go, Mom. They are waiting to help you cross over." My mother's eyebrows moved upward in acknowledgement in a surprised way. I kissed her and told her it was okay to go.

As I peered into the other side, the colors took my breath away. Many of them were similar to what we have here on earth, but some were indescribable. They were vibrant and encompassing colors. My new favorite color is on the other side.

The colors were alive, much like the plants, whose life one could feel pulsating within them, as if you had become one with the plants. The grass was about four inches in length and pointed, yet soft. Although the source of light was from a non-visible source, it adequately lit the area, as if the light emitted from the atmosphere itself. It was not blinding, nor did it glare from any direction. No need for sunglasses.

The lighting was similar to being in the shade or like the end of the day/late afternoon. The sky was medium to light blue with a slight purple hue, and appeared more vibrant than ours. I did not see any clouds or sunshine.

The scene beyond the crowd was that of a picnic-type family reunion under a large tree willow tree. There was a creek nearby and white tablecloth gently flowing in the breeze, covering a picnic table. There was no food.

As I sat there, engrossed, trying to take in everything that I could see, I smiled. How could I not? I was drawn in by the love that flowed from the other side. The love was familiar, and I have missed that feeling greatly here on earth. There are no words to describe the feeling that filled the room.

In the distance were sloping hills covered in grass and flowers. I had never seen such a beautiful scene before in my life. It was hard to stop looking at it. I was drawn to it.

I started to notice multiple spirits huddling around each other in a circle next to the head of my mother's bed. They appeared as if they were in a football huddle, with a double layer of beings encircled. They looked like a peony bud just getting ready to bloom.

The spirits remained huddled for about a minute. They seemed to be holding something and stabilizing it. Then they stood upward, and there was my mother, standing in the very center.

I rejoiced with them as my mother beamed. She appeared so happy to see everyone. It was like a vacation for her. She embraced my sister Robin several times, and then her mother. She was the celebrity in that moment, as one after the other, spirits came forward to greet and welcome her home.

In that moment, I wanted to come along too. I didn't want to be dead; I just wanted to partake in the joyous occasion of her homecoming for the day.

As I watched the festivities, and felt the love and joy that exuded from them, I could not help but smile. Then I looked down at my mom's body lying in the hospice bed and realized she had stopped breathing.

My mother has just passed away and I am sitting here smiling, I thought.

But I could not help it, as I sat there watching the events going on at her bedside.

I caught myself as I realized how it would look to another person walking into the room, to find me grinning from ear to ear when my mother had just died. They could not see what I was seeing, or know that to me my mother was not dead. They would not see she was standing on the other side of her bed with her soul very much alive.

Only about fifteen minutes elapsed between informing my mom that Gramma and Robin were there and her time to go.

I called the nurse and informed her that my mother had stopped breathing. Two nurses entered the room, walking obliviously through the souls and festivities I was witnessing. They pronounced her dead and gave me their condolences.

The festivities continued as if the nurses were not there.

When the nurses left, I remained in the room. I continued to watch the reception going on at my mother's bedside. In that moment, I could see her as plain as day standing in the crowd. She appeared so happy. I glanced over to her lifeless body that once housed her beautiful spirit. It had started to gray as the blood had stopped flowing through it.

I reflected on her life. Life had never been easy for her. She deserved so much better than what she chose for herself. I remembered her saying that she often felt like she had gotten off on the wrong planet. Now I was seeing her very much alive and the happiest I had ever seen her. I was thrilled for her to finally be at peace. No more struggling and no more pain.

From that day forward, I never mourned my mother's death, or anyone else's, for that matter. I felt that it would be selfish on my part to hold her here – to me she was not dead. How could I miss her when she is with me all the time?

Some time passed, and after about twenty minutes, the spiritual crowd thinned out. There were about eight souls left, some angelic looking and some very tall. They started to exit my mother's room. I never before understood the meaning of opening a window when someone passes away. I thought it was superstition. However, the spirits filed out one by one past my left to the window behind me and exited. The window was not vented or open; nevertheless, that was the direction that they headed.

As they passed, many leaned towards me and touched the top of my head; it felt tingly. My mother was the fourth one to pass. Still in her patient gown, I recognized her pretty shaped legs and feet from underneath the gown coming towards me. She leaned in and kissed my head, then went on.

I sat a little longer and called my siblings to notify them of our mother's passing. I again hid my joy and composed myself. Then I went to the nurses' station and spoke with the nurses to confirm that my mother's arrangements for her body had been made.

I went back to her room and kissed her cheek a final time, realizing the finality of never being able to kiss her cheek again.

I walked out of the building to my car. I thanked the Lord for taking my mother home. I cried in my car; they were a combination of tears of loss and of joy. Then I drove the hour home to tell my children and make funeral arrangements.

Since this is a topic that affects us all, why do most people avoid talking about it? Most people dread the topic – they prefer to put the conversation off until it is almost too late or until a death actually happens. Yet death is a fact of life here on this plane as we know it. We usually die only once in a lifetime, though there have been people who have had near death experiences. It can be natural or sudden, but when final death occurs, it ends the chapter.

Often when one's hearing declines in the third dimension, it is earth as it begins to open into the fifth dimension, which is heaven's frequency. Heaven's frequency cannot be measured with third dimensional instruments. The third dimensional instruments only detect the decline of hearing with both tones and sounds. As people age, the frequency to hear humans and earthly sounds reduces but all together never changes. It simply opens hearing receptors in the brain and makes one able to hear fifth dimensional conversations. These are often ignored or not spoken of until a soul gets closer to their time to cross over.

When the transitioning soul starts to talk about Uncle Charlie, who died five years ago, sitting in the corner of the room, the on looking family members often feel uncomfortable with the presence they cannot see. They try to correct the transitioning soul by saying there is no one there, or get the nurse to medicate, as we saw with Abigail and Edna.

These visuals are mistakenly called hallucinations by people who are unaware of the necessity of these visitations. If it really were hallucinations, then why would the transitioning soul still see them even after being medicated? The transitioning loved one is not talking about pink elephants climbing the walls. They are talking to spirits that others in the room also know from this lifetime.

This is an opportunity for earthbound souls to join in the elation. They may even be fortunate enough to visit with others through the transitioning member. This opportunity to communicate with the other side is often missed because spectators are afraid of death. Many people are creeped out by the transitioning soul talking about deceased loved ones being in the room.

When there is spiritual conversation going on in the room, this is a time embodied souls can also join in the conversation and communicate with spirits on the other side themselves. People often don't realize this can even be done, and miss this opportunity during their grieving.

This is an opportunity for the embodied soul to say 'hello' again to loved ones on the other side and actually get a response. The transitioning soul has the ability to hear telepathically the same as they can hear the embodied people talking in their room. Every soul on both sides can join in on the reunion of souls awaiting the embodied soul's transition.

How many times have you or someone else said that you wish you could just talk to your deceased mother, child, father, spouse etc. one more time? Or you wish you could tell them you're sorry or that you love them one more time. Perhaps you have a question for someone who has crossed over, like where did Uncle Joe put the clock? This is your chance!

Keep in mind the spirit you want to address needs to be present at the time of asking, and only one question can be asked at a time by one person at a time. If anyone else in the room is overly emotional, they may want to step out, as the frequency of the spirits is higher than ours here on earth and can increase any current emotion.

Emotions must remain balanced while communicating. Try not to freak out when you get a response. Treasure this opportunity and make what you ask important. Your questions may be limited by the transitioning soul falling asleep or medical staff coming in and out of the room.

Chapter 4

The Physical Phases of Dying

There are three types of death: Natural, Sudden and Near Death. I will start with natural death. Multiple things occur during the process of dying in a natural death. They are seen and unseen, physical and spiritual. On the physical side, from a medical standpoint, dying has multiple stages. Some people have a very gradual decline while others will transition quickly. Sometimes embodied loved ones will purposely linger until a specific person arrives to their bedside.

Natural Expected Death

According to hospice (and which I have found to be consistent in my experience), there are three phases to natural death: the pre-active phase, the active phase, and the final phase.

The pre-active phase starts approximately three weeks prior to death. The dying person may become increasingly restless and irritated. They may become agitated and harder to keep content in one position, or they don't want to be moved or gotten out of bed. Their appetite declines and they often have incontinence of bowel and bladder. They want to be alone to rest and withdraw from social activities. Sleep occurs more during the day because of being up frequently during the night. The night seems to bring on anxiety, causing them to request frequent trips to the bathroom, even though they already went minutes before.

The active phase usually occurs one to three days before death. They nap more, they may not want food or drink, and sometimes they withdraw from people and things they enjoy. Your loved one may tell others that they are going home, and it is their time. The body transitions more rapidly as the organs start to shut down. Urine decreases, and they are in and out of awareness. Their blood pressure lowers. Most people know when they are dying, and they are at peace with it. Some by this time are even looking forward to it. They know whatever the outcome, they will be okay.

As the dying process progresses to hours before their death, their skin on their legs, feet, and hands turns a mottled bluish-purple. The mottling can spread to any dependent areas of the body; for example, if the loved one is lying on their back, the mottling may also appear there and the back of their legs. Mottling is very distinct when it happens. It appears honeycomb shaped. The honeycomb-like centers are about the size of a nickel. Mottling is not painful and occurs when the heart can no longer pump blood adequately.

Sometimes they will run a low-grade fever due to lack of fluids and have a fruity acetone smell to their breath. They stop urinating and having bowel movements.

On a spiritual level, the souls on the other side are preparing a grand homecoming reunion. Deceased loved ones and friends gather to greet the person when they return home. It is a joyous occasion. The veil that separates our plane from theirs starts to efface. Movement can be seen through the now translucent veil. On one end, an entryway starts to open gradually, usually up near the head of the person's bed.

The loved one will start to close their eyes either fully or half-mast. The eye itself takes on a glazed over appearance. This does not mean they are unconscious; they can still hear you and feel your touch. Your loved one may drift in and out of consciousness. The episodes of consciousness are called 'rallying.' During the unconscious episodes, they are visiting the other side then returning. When they return, their eyes open and become bright. If they haven't been doing so already, they might start talking to others in the room that cannot be seen.

When unconsciousness returns, they lay quiet, usually with their mouth open; they are no longer able to verbalize. But again, they can feel touch if they stay to the end and can hear you, whether they are still in the physical body or in spirit standing next to you at the bedside. Some choose to stay in their body until their last breath. Others leave around the time of their last rally and their physical body is left without a soul to complete its cycle.

During this time, breathing is interrupted by gasping and slows. There might be periods of apnea, which is a longer period between breaths. The abdomen appears to overinflate with each breath instead of normal inflation in the chest area. This is called belly breathing. Often it is more of a heaving breath with mouth open. The respirations can take on a rattling sound due to saliva and mucus buildup in the throat. This happens because the swallowing reflex is one of the first things to stop functioning. Pulse and heartbeat are irregular or hard to feel or hear. Nail beds and ear lobes become pale or bluish.

It is a good idea to use oxygen as a comfort measure to avoid cramping in one's legs and medication to dry up the secretions. Oral fluids should not be given at this time. However, the mouth can be swabbed to keep it moist. Most facilities offer lemon glycerin swabs. Other things can be used. My mother's favorite beverage was diet coke, and my father's was iced tea. I opted to use those. I knew the diet coke and iced tea would be more palatable for them than the lemon. However, they must be used sparingly so as not to go into the throat and down into their lungs. When the swallowing reflex is gone, any fluid can directly go into the lungs. These are not life-sustaining measures; they are just for comfort. The patient will usually have their eyes closed partially or fully, mouth open and their breathing more labored at this time.

As I mentioned before, when a person gets closer to their bodies death/rebirth, the veil between dimensions starts to efface. This process continues as the veil becomes more translucent and partly opens, allowing souls of the transitioning loved one to start entering one at a time. The soul that enters first is usually a close relative or friend. They will be the one to call the transitioning soul home.

The veil then completely opens, and all are waiting to greet the person once they leave their body for the final time.

Pets are also in there waiting to greet their arriving loved one. However, they are not in the initial group. They join into a later reunion with the deceased soul.

The heart has stopped, and breathing has ceased. The skin takes on a yellowish appearance. The body becomes flaccid. The soul is now out of their body, not to return. The transitioned loved one is assisted by loved ones with getting used to their spiritual feet. Then, one by one, each soul approaches to greet and welcome home the departed. The newly-crossed over soul is smiling and enjoying the reunion. This reunion often continues for about twenty minutes our time in the physical realm.

After the spirits on the other side greet the new arrival, they go back to what they were doing before. The welcoming party reduces down to about five or six souls exiting with the deceased.

Sudden Death

The difference between dying suddenly without notice, in often traumatic circumstances, and dying with notice and letting life take its natural course, is the way in which the soul reacts to the death. Sudden death can be both natural, as in a heart attack, and tragic, as in a murder. What happens when death is abrupt and unexpected?

When death is sudden and unexpected, most times the spirit is catapulted out of the body right before the cause of death occurs, if death is imminent. The soul itself often goes though minutes to days of disbelief, and sometimes denial. Often they do not realize they have died. The souls will even stand next to their body watching paramedics working to save their lives, trying to crawl back into their body.

This has been verified by people who have had near death experiences. They have a feeling of *this cannot be*! This often leaves the spirit in a state of shock and panic, more so for adults then children – children are less bothered by what's happening because they so recently came from the other side. Adults, however, sometimes cling to their body until the last minute. They know that something has happened. They can see the cause of death or even their own dead body. They can hear the medical team talking and they feel the sheet being put over their face or bag zippered. Sometimes they are in disbelief and run about seeking help. They go through a process similar to the steps of grieving: denial, bargaining, and acceptance.

The soul's thoughts race about all of the things they needed to finish. They are worried about their loved ones left behind and what they will do when they hear of the spirit's death, as well as unfinished business that they need to attend to. They worry about their pets and children and who's going to take care of them. They even worry about little things, like where they have hidden valuables, and hope that someone will find them before the item is donated or thrown out. They also worry about the things they should have done but never got around to, such as wills, cashing a check, life insurance, etc.

They also worry about not getting to say goodbye to their loved ones. This is an emotional period that needs to settle first before entry onto the other side. The spirit guides' vibration is so high that it can make a situation become more intense, whether good or bad. Therefore, the spirit guides linger in the distance, watching and waiting for the soul to calm down enough to be approached.

The spirit or spirits sent to assist will then stay with them. The soul is given the choice to cross over or not. Once the soul has accepted their death and agreed to cross over, they are assisted with closure; the dead soul visits loved ones left behind on earth. They are also allowed a glimpse into the future to show the loved ones left behind will be okay with the newly deceased soul gone. Often the loved one reports seeing the newly deceased at their bedside or during a twilight sleep. This may take several of our earthly days to complete. Once completed, and the soul feels ready, they are guided to and welcomed with a homecoming as grand as usual.

It is very important to let the spirit know, regardless of the way they passed, that it is okay for them to go home. The spirit will make a lot more visits preceding death to loved ones to check in and see everyone.

Once the spirit crosses over, they can come back and forth between planes and will come when thought of or called. With one difficulty: when people on the earthly plane mourn too long, it creates a vacuum, anchoring part of the spirit earthbound. They need to be released completely. They are not really dead. And it isn't the last time you will see them.

Let's put it into a different perspective. Try to think of your lost loved one as being on vacation. You will miss them and look forward to seeing them again, but the forlorn emotion of grief that is normal to feel will not go on too long. It's healthier for the deceased, as well as the loved ones left behind.

Dead on Arrival

I took my three-year-old daughter Ivy to the grocery store to pick up a few things. It was dark outside and had been raining all day, making the roads wet and slippery. After leaving the grocery store, I started to head home.

On the way home, we had to pull over three times to allow two fire trucks and ambulances to pass through. I remember thinking there must have been a bad accident ahead. I hoped no one was hurt.

As I came around the bend, I observed blaring lights from first responders to an automobile accident. A car had collided with a semi-truck hauling gasoline. The gas truck had been making a wide turn into a gas station, taking up two lanes. The car driving in the lane that the truck was blocking went underneath the trailer part of the truck. The top of the car was peeled back, and the police were redirecting traffic and taping off the area.

While Ivy and I sat, waiting to pass in the lane the police had opened, Ivy said to me, "Mommy, look at the man. He's wearing ketchup on his face."

"What man?" I asked.

"The one looking at me in my window," she responded.

I looked over my shoulder and caught a glimpse in my peripheral vision of a frantic older man near Ivy's back seat window. When I looked at him directly, there was nothing there. I recognized this as an entity that had not crossed over yet. He appeared to have blood on his face.

It was obvious that he had been involved in the accident in some way.

He walked away to another idle car behind us.

Later that evening, there was a news broadcast about the accident. There had been a fatality: an older man.

Once the newly-deceased has gone through the stages of grief – the first stage being denial, then bargaining for more time, and finally acceptance – they are then approached by a familiar spirit from the other side.

Suicide

One is supposed to leave this plane when it is their agreed time. They chose the time and the way they will die before they entered this plane. There are five opportunities for death within one's lifetime. The ways we can die are also prearranged, including being murdered by someone.

Suicide is not ever an option or considered one of the pre-planned exits from life. It is a serious offense on multiple dimensional planes. It is perceived as murder of oneself. We have a contract, so to speak, of what we have come to this plane to assist with or accomplish. We are also an important piece to other people's goals and life paths. We are relying on each other to be there. Your parents, your children and neighbors, lovers, friends, and the kid who mows your lawn or babysits, even the homeless man you met are all connected, each with a purpose in one's life, even if it is hardly recognizable.

Sometimes we never get to know the outcomes until we cross over. Then we find out the homeless person who we paused to give a bottle of water saved us from an accident just waiting to happen a few seconds down the road. He was placed in the path at that moment to slow us down and prevent a tragedy. Sometimes angels come in many forms. They don't always appear perfect and beautiful; like the bully who teaches another not to be one, because of being bullied.

We choose what we set out to accomplish for our own education and retribution. We have chosen the people we have come into this life with to accomplish our goals. We picked our parents, regardless of how good or bad they have been.

If we do not meet our goals, we will repeat schooling on the other side, and then on to the third dimension again in similar circumstances. Earth is not an easy school ground. We are all placed here specifically to learn how to raise our vibrations and get back to a perfect loving, selfless state of being.

Not only are we chosen to be in our life on earth, we also volunteered. We are chosen by our source, or God, out of a chosen group. We then volunteer and one out of our group is chosen.

Suicide is not supposed to ever be an option. It is an insult to others who could have come into life, in your place, and completed the job you prematurely exited on. You didn't have to come into this lifetime. It's an honor and you requested it.

When one commits suicide, it is expected and sudden. They feel the physical pain that causes the death, which is traumatic in itself. Then there is discomfort as the physical body fights to remain alive; it knows its time is not completed. One will experience the suffering either right before death or in their life review.

The newly-deceased soul, after the suicide is committed, doesn't go through the trauma of an unexpected death. When suicide has been committed for selfish, spiteful, or senseless reasons, the soul is collected by a higher being instead of a familiar friend or loved one. They are taken immediately for a life review that includes the rippling effect of their poor decision to end their life contract early.

They are made aware how it has adversely affected others who came into this lifetime counting on them to be there so others can also accomplish their goals. They are made to feel the intense, agonizing emotional suffering they have caused each individual they have left behind. They are made aware of what they missed out on in the future and the adverse effects it had on other goals.

They are shown what their contract was and are sent back to schooling to understand how severe their actions were. They continue school until completed, then are sent back into the family group they left behind to complete their contract or into a very similar situation with a paralleling family on earth. (I specify "earth" because there are other solar systems with earth-like planets and inhabitants.) They can return by rebirth as a baby or a walk-in. A walk-in is where two souls agree to switch places, or one ascends in order to allow the soul being sent back to re-enter life in a body. The ascending soul is at one of its five exit opportunities and leaves. The soulless body then becomes a cavity for the awaiting spirit to inhabit.

The soul will again live up to the same point, in similar circumstances, at which they committed suicide in their previous life. They can choose not to do so this time, cope in a different, hopefully heathier way, and complete their life goals. However, this time will be harder because they will not have all of the support that was originally sent to the life they left prematurely. Many of these souls are put back into circulation to re-enter life in similar conditions very quickly. They do not get a grand reception. They usually are not even allowed to see loved ones while on the other side. Suicide is a very serious offense that affects life in our plane, and the other side, as well. It is not rewarded until one's contract is fulfilled.

Souls of those who ended their own lives are not sent to Hell! Although having to bear the burden that they caused and the judgement they place on themselves may make them wish they could go south instead. Returning prematurely is not pleasant.

However, in the case of suicide because of severe depression, significant mental illness, or malevolent attachment, the process is different. The soul is approached by a higher being and given the option to return home or go back into a life cycle. If they choose to stay home, they are cocooned for a period of time to rest, then they are reunited with loved ones without the grand reception, and schooled.

They are schooled by being placed to assist an earthly being who is suicide-prone to get help before it goes that far. If they choose to return after being cocooned, they are also schooled before being sent back. Either way, suicide is not a good thing.

Near Death Experiences

During each person's lifetime, there are several openings to the fifth dimension where we can choose to leave and cross over at that time or stay on earth. If we pass one of those time frames, we then stay until the next opportunity. That is why some who do not fall into those time frames are sent back; since it is not yet their time. Our final breath is predetermined prior to birth and is given in earth time a three-day window. The day is known but not necessarily the hour. Souls have been known to fight death while waiting for a particular family member or friend to arrive, as well as the birth of a baby or graduation they really wanted to be an embodied part of.

Ray

Ray went to his doctor for an annual physical. He was in good shape and had no signs or symptoms that would indicate anything being wrong health-wise. During the exam, however, the doctor noticed bulging vessels in Ray's left eye. The doctor became greatly concerned and sent Ray straight from the doctor's office to the emergency room for tests.

The test results showed Ray had a large clot in his carotid artery. The doctor noticed the clot was traveling towards his brain.

"There is nothing to be done," the doctor told Ray, "for a clot that size and so close to your brain, other than surgery. You'll be dead within twenty-four hours from a massive stroke if we don't remove the clot."

Ray was taken straight from the emergency room to the operating room. It all happened so fast Ray didn't even have a chance to call any of his children to notify them of what was taking place. He only had time to call his new bride, Larysa, and notify her.

Ray was in surgery within sixty-five minutes of walking into the door of the emergency room. The surgery took about an hour. He was taken to the recovery room.

Ray became aware of his surroundings in the recovery room as he started to awaken. The nurse had just taken his blood pressure and noticed he was waking.

"Your blood pressure is good," she told him.

After the nurse removed the blood pressure cuff, she proceeded to check Ray's IV and clean the port.

"What his pain level, on a scale of one to ten?" the nurse asked Ray. "One being no pain and ten being the most painful thing you can remember."

"A six," Ray responded.

The nurse inserted the syringe into the port and started to dispense the solution from the syringe directly into the IV line.

"What is that?" Ray asked.

"This is just a little morphine to help with the pain," the nurse replied.

Ray had an ominous feeling come over him and an overwhelming urge to say, "NO!" to the morphine. Through his grogginess, he blurted, "No, I don't want that!"

"You don't want any pain medicine?" the nurse replied, as she removed the now-empty syringe from the IV-line port.

"No morphine!" Ray replied.

In the meantime, the surgeon went to the waiting room to tell Ray's wife the procedure had gone well. Ray's wife was relieved and told the doctor, "Thank you."

While standing there, the doctor's pager went off. As he looked at it, an announcement came over the hospital's PA system announcing a code blue in the recovery room. The doctor excused himself and asked Ray's wife to wait there.

"I want to make rounds on your husband in the recovery room," the doctor said.

He left quickly while dialing his phone to the recovery room. Ray's wife sat back down and waited. She was feeling relieved the surgery went well.

Little did she know, but the code blue was for Ray.

Ray had a history of low blood pressure and was unaware that he was allergic to morphine. He had never used it before. Morphine as a drug tends to reduce respirations and lower blood pressure. After the injection into his IV-line, he went into cardiac arrest. Ray could feel himself weightlessly floating upwards toward the ceiling. He turned over while floating and saw the nurse running to the phone in the recovery room to order a code blue. Ray could hear a code being called over the PA system in the recovery room. He watched as nurses and doctors filled the room and initiated CPR and other measures on his lifeless body. As he watched, he continued upward toward the ceiling. He lingered in the room, yet he also had the sensation of actively standing next to each one of his children at the same time. He also was with Larysa and could feel her concern as she waited to see if the code blue was for him. He was six different places equally at one time.

Ray's soul then went through the ceiling and quickly propelled upward. He rolled over to look upward and realized he was in what seemed to be a tunnel, almost like outer space had wrapped itself around him. The feeling of euphoria made it quite pleasant inside. The dark yet shimmering gold speckled atmosphere bathed his soul in its warmth and unconditional love. The gold shimmering star-like particles floated softly around him. The feeling of love was like nothing he had experienced on earth until that moment. He realized how much he had missed and longed for this feeling.

Ray could see a light at the end of the tunnel. His movement slowed towards the opening, and then paused. During this pause, he became very aware of the beings around him. They were both in the distance and nearby. The ones in the distance he somehow knew where other souls like him that were completing their earthbound lives and were on their journey home. The ones nearer by were magnificent heavenly beings. He saw a group of them standing together facing each other as if they were in a conversation.

One of the beings approached him and stood in midair on a cloudlike mist. The others disappeared into a mist as if a curtain had closed. Yet the curtain was still transparent enough to see movement on the other side of it and an occasional face or limb peek through.

The male soul that approached Ray wore a white robe-like garment that was belted with a golden cord and tied at his waist. The man had slightly wavy, pearlescent white hair about two inches past his shoulder. It glistened as if fiber optics were in it. He had a neatly maintained beard with a mustache. His eyes were a bright bluish purple.

The soul spoke to Ray from his mind to Ray's mind. Ray would later recount this experience and explain that thoughts are transparent for all to see on the other side. Thinking there is like talking is here. Our thought patterns go out into the universe, up to heaven/the other side, even stronger than our words. Ray said standing with this being was a humbling experience. This being was familiar to him. He knew that this angelic being had been with him throughout every step of his life on earth.

The heavenly being conveyed to Ray that they were stopping his journey home there and that he would have a decision to make. He explained to Ray that in our life on earth, there are several times during an earthly lifetime that one has the opportunity to exit and come home. It is often a choice made in our subconscious, whether we are acutely aware of it or not. These opportunities are usually not remembered by the earthbound souls.

The being reminded Ray of two instances when he could have come home early but chose not to. Once was when Ray was in a car accident. The other time, he fell from his ladder. He was told those were portals to exit if he had wanted to.

The heavenly being went on to explain that we have made an agreement or contract before we come here to accomplish certain things in one's lifetime.

"We on the other side understand the difficulty of life on earth," he conveyed, "therefore, we have given this option to naturally exit and cross back over by causes not intentionally created."

The heavenly being pointed upward at the mist above him and Ray, and as Ray watched, he was able to review his life as if he were watching television. He felt every pain and joy his actions created in his lifetime and the long-term effects his actions created for his loved ones and pets.

Ray cried a lot during his review. It started from his birth and finished at present day. He could barely stand to look at much of it. He could feel himself falling to his knees begging for forgiveness and the opportunity to make things right. He had been unaware of all the sorrow he had caused others. He had also been unaware of all the opportunities and events he missed out on or didn't remember because of his alcoholism.

Shortly after the movie of his life finished playing, the being told Ray that he was being given a choice to continue to the light or return to earth. He was then shown another visual, only this time it was of current day. Ray was able to look upon his five children. It was as if he was standing right next to each of them. He visited them simultaneously and knew that all of them would be okay if he chose to continue to the other side. Most of his children were estranged due to his actions towards them. He was saddened that they would never know how much he loved them and regretted any harm he had caused.

He then viewed his Russian bride, who did not know how to drive yet or even how to balance a checkbook. She still needed him to finish up some things with her.

Ray chose to return to earth.

Upon that decision, Ray felt his soul swiftly descending. He came through the clouds into the hospital ceiling and stopped as he entered the room. He rolled over and saw the doctors and nurses working on his corpse. He rolled over, facing the ceiling, and was gently sucked back into his body.

In that moment, he laid there and felt the weightiness of his body, like a one-hundred-eighty-pound wet blanket. He felt the overwhelming pain from both the surgery and the injuries he endured during the efforts to resuscitate him. Ray opened his eyes and took a deep breath.

The doctor called out, "We have a pulse!

"Welcome back," he said to Ray. "We thought we had lost you."

The doctor remained with Ray until he stabilized and was transferred to the intensive care unit. Then he once again went to the waiting area to inform Ray's wife of what had happened, and that Ray was now stable and would need to be monitored.

Ray entrusted me with his story after hearing mine about my haunted house. He told me he had never spoken of it before until now.

After explaining all that had happened, Ray went so far as to describe what his daughter Lori was wearing that day. They lived in different states and were estranged. What he described was her favorite outfit; she wore it a lot. However, he had never seen it before. He said he knew that if he had chosen to cross over, that each of his children would be okay. However, he knew that his new bride from Russia would still need some help acclimating to life in America, so when given a choice, he chose to return.

Ray said that heavenly love encompasses one's soul. It washes away all suffering and fills one with joy that is unimaginable on earth. The intensity is comfortable and nourishing to the soul. One does not realize how negative and exhausting life is here on earth until they have experienced death.

"When my time comes to cross over," Ray said, "I will embrace it. And if given a choice again, I will not return to earth."

He lived ten more years. During that time, he made all the arrangements for his future passing, even wrote out his own obituary, a list of where to call for pensions and stocks for his wife, and taught his bride how to drive. He paid off their house and made sure everything was in order for her. He quit drinking after being a severe alcoholic for seventy years. He made amends for his mistakes with his family and apologized to people that deserved to get an apology from him. Ray was not an easy man. He had been a physically abusive tyrant most of his life.

However, his near death experience humbled him greatly. He was quite different in an exceptionally good way afterwards. Ray felt good about the condition he was going to leave everyone he loved in. He made every day count. He loved more, and sought out others, making opportunities to make a positive difference in another's life.

On October 3 of 2017, Ray crossed over peacefully in the early morning from complications of vocal cord cancer. He had been diagnosed two months earlier. The evening before he crossed over for the final time, he went through periods of entering and exiting his body. Upon his soul reentering, he would open his eyes and speak of seeing his deceased mother and grandmother. He spoke to them and claimed they were in the room. His wife would correct him and tell him no one was there. He insisted and she told him he was hallucinating.

When Larysa left the room, Lori approached Ray and told him he was in fact seeing the people he had mentioned, and that his wife couldn't understand because she was unable to see them, too. He lay quietly, mouthing words with no sound, smiling at times as if he was enjoying the conversation with the beings he was communicating with.

Ray waited for everyone to leave and go home before taking his last breath. It was his wish to be alone and not have people crying over his death. Ray understood that grieving keeps the soul earthly-connected. The act of releasing helps the soul to cross over. There is a difference between sadness of a loss and grieving, and missing someone and grieving, according to Ray.

He did not want a funeral, either. He wanted a celebration. He wanted his family to meet on the beach that he went to almost every day to celebrate his crossing over and release his ashes into the ocean, where they would swim forever. He wanted Pink Floyd's "Off the Wall" to be played (one would have to understand Ray's dry sense of humor to understand that one) while his loved ones ate his favorite potato salad on the beach.

Ray's spirit pops in every once in a while, to make his presence known.

Lily

For children things are a bit different. Children can see inter-dimensionally. Since they have so recently come from the other side, the veil between dimensions is thin for them, and in some places still open, allowing them to see the other side simultaneously. As a child grows, the veil thickens and closes. For them, death is simply like walking home. Children are not afraid of death.

When near death experiences happen for children, they often speak of crossing over a bridge in a beautifully flowered meadow, or they speak of a rainbow bridge. They are always guided by someone familiar, either someone who has crossed over from the child's current lifetime or a soul they recognize from before they came to earth. We have family on both sides – some awaiting entry, some who have returned, and others who remain on the other side. We reunite with those once we cross over.

Lily drowned when she was four years old. Her family was at a hotel. In the early morning hours, her father was making trips back and forth to the car, loading it and getting ready for the family to check out and leave. Lily's mother was feeling a bit overwhelmed as she tended the baby sister while trying to get Lily and her brother dressed, as well as herself dressed and ready to go.

Lily's father encouraged Lily and her brother Ryan to follow along with him while he loaded the car. Each of her father's three trips went past the hotel swimming pool. Lily and Ryan trailed behind their father each time.

On the third trip past the pool, Lily's dad walked faster, leaving Ryan and Lily behind. The two were slowing him down, as they would pause to look at flowers and things along the way.

Lily and Ryan neared the pool. No one was around. It was still somewhat dark outside. The sun was just starting to come up.

There was a puddle next to the pool left from the sprinklers. Lily was wearing flip flops that were slippery on the bottom.

Ryan began teasing Lily, threatening to tickle her. Lily quickly pulled away from Ryan to avoid being tickled. She slipped in the puddle and fell into the deep end of the pool.

Lily began going down under the water. While sinking down, she observed the drain in the pool under the water. The water was not visually clear, and she became scared that the drain might suck her in. Lily felt cold from the temperature of the water and tried to reach her foot out, hoping to feel the side of the pool so she could push off of it, thinking it would help her get to the surface. But she could not swim or reach the sides of the pool. She floated in the deep water near the bottom of the pool, not knowing what to do.

When she looked up, she saw a bright light that became larger and brighter as it came closer. Just then, things under water suddenly appeared clear, as if she had an underwater mask on. Lily was no longer cold; comforting warmth encircled her. She glanced back at the drain and started to cry, wondering why no one was coming to get her out.

Lily saw light emitting from above – then a beautiful young woman dove into the pool. Lily later described the woman as having long dark brown hair past her waist. The woman grabbed Lily's hand and pulled her out and away from the pool.

Lily and this magnificent being both hovered over the pool, hand in hand. They were floating in midair. Lily could still see her body in the pool under the water. She felt comforted by the woman's presence.

Lily noticed all of a sudden that her clothes and hair were dry. She noticed the woman's clothes and hair appeared dry, too, even though they had both just gotten out of the pool.

Lily pulled on her own shirt and asked the woman why her clothes were dry.

"Watch!" the woman replied.

Lily was very content standing with the woman, hand in hand. She felt the love encompassing her from the woman, who felt remarkably familiar, like she had known her forever.

Next thing Lily knew, she now stood at the opposite end of the pool with the woman. She really liked the woman and wanted to stay with her.

Lily heard sirens coming closer.

The two watched a man leaning over a child's body while two other men in white shirted uniforms arrived with the sirens.

The woman told Lily, "Watch," a second time.

The man leaning over the child was Lily's father. He had been a paratrooper medic in World War II. He immediately started resuscitative measures on Lily's small body at poolside.

Lily woke up on the ground. She lay on a towel, with another towel rolled up behind her head. She was coughing and choking and saw her father over her. Her chest burned as the water exited her lungs.

She raised her arm up to touch her hair and noticed it was wet. Then she felt her clothes; they were very wet, too. Lily started to look for the woman who had been holding her hand. But she was gone.

"Where did the lady go?" Lily asked.

She asked over and over for the woman who had gotten her out of the pool, but no one seemed to know who she was talking about. No one else had seen her.

Later on, Lily talked about the woman often. She told of how the lady with bright blue eyes and dark hair would still come and see her on occasion, and about the games they played together. Lily's parents told her no one was there playing with her, and it was all her imagination. But Lily knew differently and was confused as to why her parents could not see the lady, too. Lily would overhear her parents talking about her stories of the lady and hoped Lily would stop talking about the woman soon. But she continued to talk about seeing this woman until she was ten years old.

Two years later, Lily became a big sister to a second younger sister. Because Lily's sister was born later in the family, she was still young when Lily got married and moved away.

When they reunited years later, Lily had a deja vu moment; her sister, now a young woman, looked identical to the beautiful young woman she remembered diving into the hotel pool and holding her hand.

Ann

Ann was a mother of one going through a divorce. She felt unattractive about her body and her breasts after breast feeding her daughter. Her husband leaving for another woman did not help her self-esteem much, either.

Ann went to a plastic surgeon for some body sculpting and a breast augmentation with mastopexy. Ann decided for her mother to come and stay with her and her four-year-old daughter for the week.

On the day of the surgery, Ann arrived early at the surgery ward in the doctor's office. The plastic surgeon drew on her breasts, hips, and inner and outer thighs with a marker for incisions to be made. Ann was readied for surgery.

The surgery went well, and Ann was discharged home. The bandages covered most of her body due to the liposuction on her hips, inner and outer thighs, and knees. She also had bandages on her breasts. Ann was in an overwhelming amount of pain.

Ann's mother administered the pain medication as prescribed by her doctor. Little did they know, but Ann was allergic to a component in the medication.

About an hour after Ann was given the medication, she could hear her mother calling her and shaking her to wake up.

Ann remembered exiting her body and floating upward quickly. She could hear her mother calling 911 and then everything went blank for a few seconds. She noticed she was floating up into the gentle darkness towards an opening.

The opening appeared as if the clouds had separated, leaving a hole. Beyond the hole was a clear blue sky. As Ann went through the opening, she was in a beautiful meadow with wildflowers blooming everywhere. Some of the flowers were thigh high. The scent was entrancing. She basked in the loving sensations she experienced.

Ann noticed some flowers she did not recognize and some colors she had never seen before. They were stunning. All of them seemed to be pulsating with life. She noticed the sky was clear and that the light, though bright, did not make her squint. It was very comfortable lighting. It was as if the light emitted from within itself, as an obvious light source was not apparent.

Ann walked along in the field toward a tree. As she got closer, there appeared to be a man kneeling near the tree. As she approached the man, he stood up and came forward. He was tall and slender, and appeared to be in his thirties with reddish curly hair.

"It is not your time," he told Ann with his mind. "You should go back."

Ann could not understand how she could hear the fellow without his mouth moving.

Sensing Ann's reluctance, the man pointed towards the sky and showed Ann her life review. She was then shown some things that were yet to occur in her life as part of the agreement she had made with other souls prior to being born onto earth. Ann was confused.

"All the people on earth are there because they chose to be," the man explained. "Most of them volunteered. Prior to each lifetime, the individuals within the life cycle family chose their parents and siblings. They also chose their sex, race, religion, financial status, children, and their significant others."

The man went on to convey that because of this fact, on the other side they do not understand why there is so much blame and accusations of prejudice on earth. Each person chose every detail of who they are in this lifetime. It serves as their educational path to enlightenment. Each of our lives has a rippling effect on the next generations preparing to be on earth and other solar systems for a life cycle.

The man then introduced himself as Ann's great grandson, who was supposed to be born into the family line from a child she had not given birth to yet.

"Will you have red hair?" Ann asked.

He smiled and said, "Yes."

At that point in her life, Ann didn't plan to ever remarry or have more children. Furthermore, she thought if she did, it would not be with anyone red headed. She preferred dark haired men.

Ann noticed out of the corner of her eye, bounding through the flowers, was her childhood dog, who was aiming straight for her, followed by another larger dog she had lost to cancer two years earlier. They both joyously greeted her. As the ground vibrated, an elephant appeared with a group of other animals. They all were her beloved pets from many lifetimes.

After spending some time reuniting with each one, Ann understood the importance of her returning and how much her little girl needed her.

Ann awakened in the ambulance on the way to the hospital. She could see the IV dripping and a red-haired paramedic. He asked her what her name was, if she knew what day it was, and who the President was, to assess her mental acuity. Ann was groggy but answered the questions correctly. Her tongue had swollen and was making it hard for her to breath. The paramedic worked hard to open her airway.

Ann was treated in the hospital and released two days later. When she went home after recuperating a few more days, her mother told Ann that she herself needed to return home.

Ann's mother prepared to leave. As she was loading her car, she tripped on a sprinkler head and twisted her ankle. Ann called 911.

And who showed up but the red headed paramedic that saved Ann's life!

Ann wanted to notify the paramedic's boss about what a great job he had done and how much she appreciated it. The paramedic gave Ann his business card so she could write a letter to his boss. She found the paramedic to be very charming.

Ann and the paramedic were married two years later and had two more children, both redheads. And those children grew to have red-headed children.

Ann passed away from cancer before her third great grandchild was born – the only red-haired great grandson.

Jason

Jason was two years old. He was outside with his dad while his dad washed his car. Jason went around to the other side of his dad's car where the large, paint-sized bucket was filled with soapy water. He went over to the bucket and dropped his hot wheel car into the water.

As he reached into the bubbly water to retrieve his car, he fell headfirst into the bucket. The father was busy detailing the tires opposite the bucket.

Jason was in the water for about three minutes when Jason's mother came outside and started screaming as she pulled his lifeless body from the bucket. The parents did not know how to do CPR and called 911.

The paramedics arrived within five minutes. Jason was resuscitated on the scene and raced to the hospital while going in and out of consciousness. He remained in the hospital for three days, being monitored and treated for aspiration pneumonia.

After coming home, Jason spoke of an angel man who went with Jason to get his mommy when Jason fell into the water. He said the angel man took him by the hand into the house and whispered to Jason's mommy, "Check on Jason."

Jason said he and the man then followed Jason's mom outside. He and Jason watched her pull Jason out of the water.

Jason remembered the ambulance arriving and his mother and father crying. He remembered feeling the sensation of burning as he breathed in the water. He also remembered not being able to make his body move and how comforted he was when the angel man came and took him out of the water.

As mentioned before, during our lifetime, there are several opportunities to cross over early. We can choose to leave and cross over at the time or to stay. If we pass one of the time frames, we then stay until the next designated opportunity, which is why some souls are sent back. It is no their time yet. This is a near death experience.

During near death experiences, only limited areas in the fifth dimension are available to the new arrival that will be sent back.

Chapter 5

Robin

Robin was a raven-haired beauty. She was elegant and refined, with long straight waist-length hair and striking blue eyes. She had a sweetness about her and she was always willing to help others. She was a great student and asset to the community. She was the youngest in her family and got spoiled a bit because of it.

Robin's parents were divorced, and she didn't get to see much of her father, as he frequently traveled abroad and stayed for months at a time. She never really dated much in high school until in her senior year, when she met a young man named Chad. He invited her to the senior prom. Robin was thrilled and accepted his offer. This invitation to the prom started a two-year relationship that appeared normal at first. It led to an engagement a year and a half later.

After high school graduation, Robin started to take classes at the local community college. She took a few core classes while she prepared to transfer to a school for architecture in the fall. Her dream was to become an architect. Robin had a talent for drawing and designing homes and buildings. She also had a flare for decorating. She was able to pull colors and details together beautifully.

Robin lived at home with her mother while she worked to save up money to buy her own car. Robin got her first job as a cashier at the local drug store. She went to school during the day and worked part-time evenings.

Chad was with her every spare minute she had. The two were inseparable.

Chad was also still living at home with his parents, and was working and making payments on his sports car. On Valentine's Day, he asked Robin to marry him and she accepted. They planned to marry when Robin finished school.

After Robin agreed to marry Chad, he convinced her to open a joint checking account with him. He reassured her that both would have access to the account and for both to put their savings into the account. Chad excused his lack of savings because of buying her engagement ring. Robin balked at the idea of putting her savings into the account, as that money had been saved by her for a car.

Chad convinced Robin they could use his car and she didn't need one right away. Robin trusted – after all, they were getting married – and opened the joint account with Chad, depositing her savings of about $2,500 into the account.

Chad and Robin discussed saving up for their wedding. They decided each would put in as much money as they could from every paycheck into the bank account. They also agree that no purchases would be taken out of the account without the other knowing. Chad convinced Robin that he needed to keep his personal checking account to make his car payments. His reasoning was that the money would not be taken from their mutual account.

Robin did not know that Chad was about to lose his job for frequently calling out of work to stalk her. Because of his lack of work, he was going to have trouble making his car payments.

Robin had been sharing a car with her mother. This made it difficult for her to attend school and get to her job. She sometimes had to pay for a ride. She never missed a class or missed a day of work, despite the difficulty.

When Chad would help out with rides, Robin knew this was also interfering with his job. Chad would never allow Robin to use his car. Instead, he insisted on dropping her off and picking her up.

Robin decided she wanted some independence. Her sister was renting a townhouse within walking distance to Robin's school and had offered for Robin to move in with her as a roommate. They would share the expenses.

The townhouse was also closer to Robin's job and had a bus stop near the entrance of the development. Robin agreed to pay one third of the rent while Lori paid the other two thirds and utilities. In this new location, not only could Robin easily catch the bus, but she could use her sister's car. Robin's sister was working midnights and slept during the day.

Chad became even more possessive as Robin became more independent. He demanded frequent contact with Robin. He had to know where she was constantly and who she was with. He would always ask if she was with a man.

On one of those days, Robin had come home from school early. Her stomach was upset and she needed to use the bathroom.

Somehow Chad knew Robin had left school early. He started calling Robin's cell phone. Robin had laid her phone down on the counter. She had then gone upstairs to use the bathroom and shower, and then lay down.

Within ten minutes, Chad started to call her phone. He called seventeen times until Lori was finally awakened by the ringing, and got up and answered it.

"You're f#&king some guy from your class," Chad raged, not realizing it was Lori who had answered the phone. "I know you have a man in your bedroom. I'm parked right outside your house."

"This is Lori," Lori responded.

"Is Robin there?" Chad asked. "Why are you answering her phone?"

"Robin is home," Lori said. "She's in the bathroom because she isn't feeling well."

Chad asked her to have Robin call him back.

When Robin returned Chad's call, Lori could hear Robin reassuring him that no men were with her, repeating it over and over.

Suddenly he was at the townhouse door, insisting to come in and prove that no men were in there. Once he entered, he ended up staying for hours, with the television blaring in Robin's room.

This living arrangement was short lived; things started to change. Lori noticed that Robin would not ask to use her car, even though Lori would leave the keys on the kitchen counter for Robin to use. Chad drove Robin to and from everywhere.

While Lori was working midnights, Chad basically moved himself into the townhouse, without permission, and without paying rent or for food. Lori started to notice some of the other bizarre behaviors Chad had towards Robin. Robin was never able to talk to Lori alone. Chad was always glued to her. He would even go so far as to insist that Robin stay all afternoon at his parents' house, with his mother home, whenever Chad had to do something away from Robin.

Even when Lori called Robin on the phone, Chad could be overheard asking Robin what Lori wanted and telling her she would not be able to stay on long, because of whatever they needed to go do, and that she needed to get off the phone.

He would not allow her to go anywhere alone with Lori. If Lori invited Robin to go out for lunch, Chad had to come along. He would answer questions asked of Robin before she even had a chance to say anything.

Lori also started to notice that when Robin was at school, a place he had to let her be alone at, Chad would be at the townhouse in Robin's room, lying around and waiting to pick Robin up.

One day, Lori was awakened from her daytime slumber and walked out of her bedroom, expecting to be home alone, since Robin was not there...only to walk out in her pajamas and be startled by Chad's presence.

Lori darted back into her room to put on a bathrobe, then came back out and asked, "Why are you not working?"

Chad replied that he was off that day.

"Why are you here?" she asked.

"I had to get something Robin needs," Chad responded, and he left.

Lori went into the kitchen. She had cleaned it the night before. It was obvious by the dishes in the sink and drying food left on the countertops that Chad had been at the townhouse for most of the day.

The third month, Robin started to have a hard time paying her part of the rent. It seemed as if once her money was deposited into her and Chad's account, she was not allowed to use it. Lori overheard Robin and Chad arguing in the bedroom about why she could not take her rent from the joint account. Chad reassured her they needed to save that money for their wedding. He told Robin that he would pay her rent when he got paid on the upcoming Friday. Friday was also Robin's payday.

Robin told Lori she would have the rent on Friday and asked if she could make payments every two weeks instead of once a month. Lori agreed. Lori fronted the rent so as to pay it on time.

When Friday came, Robin came crying to Lori, handing her the rent money and saying that was all the money she had. It was $35, half of the agreed biweekly amount of $75.

"Didn't you get paid today?" Lori asked.

"Yes," Robin cried, "but this $35, most of which was in change, is all I have, and it leaves me with nothing for food for the week."

This deeply concerned Lori. She felt something was not right, but could not ask more because Chad was standing there. Lori handed the money back to Robin, but she refused to take it.

The next day, Lori found two wadded up important-looking papers in the bathroom trash can. She picked each up and straightened them out. One was a notice to repossess Chad's car. He was in arrears three months, totaling over $1000 with late fees and penalties. The second was his VISA statement, showing he was over the limit and had not made a payment on the card for three months. He owed $2000 that would have to be paid to reinstate the card.

Lori suspected Chad was lying about working and Robin was being drained of the money she was making in order to pay for his expenses. She waited for them to arrive at the townhouse.

Lori told Chad he was not allowed to stay overnight at the townhouse anymore and that he needed to go home to his parents. She knew it was the only way to get Robin separated from him long enough to tell Robin what she had found and suspected about Chad.

He became enraged. Lori stood firm and told him she was not responsible for him and that he does not pay rent, utilities or even wash his dishes to live there.

"Robin does!" Chad retorted.

"Yes," Lori said, "for her, not for you, too."

Chad demanded Robin leave with him that evening. He returned her late.

He went home that night, but then showed up at 5:00 am, and unbeknownst to Lori, awakened Robin and coerced her to let him inside. He went into Robin's bedroom, where he stayed quiet and hidden.

Lori had a meeting that morning and stopped briefly at Robin's bedroom door to see if she needed a ride to school that morning.

"No," she said.

She sounded as if she had been crying.

"Are you okay?" Lori asked. "Do you want me to fix you breakfast?"

"No," Robin said.

"Okay," Lori said. "I love you."

Then she left.

When Lori arrived back home, she noticed Chad's car parked out of the way in a parking space on the other side of the complex's pool.

"I wonder why Chad parked all the way over there when parking spaces are available right in front of our townhouse?" she wondered to herself.

When Lori entered her home, Robin was upstairs with Chad in her room. Lori did not hear a peep out of them for hours until they both came downstairs, leaving to take Robin to work. Occasionally Robin would respond to Lori's goodbye, but Chad would not speak.

Lori had to work the next four nights.

The first morning Lori came home, Chad pulled up right behind her and said he was there to pick up Robin. He came in and went straight up to Robin's room. An hour later they came downstairs. Robin would not even look Lori in the eye.

"Good morning," Lori said.

Robin responded a muffled "goodbye" and off they went.

Lori had a churning feeling in her gut. She called Robin's cell phone and left a message that she needed to talk to her in private and for her to call back. Robin did not return the call.

The next two nights, when Lori got home from work, it looked as if someone had just pulled out of her parking space. The dew was moist on the ground and the sprinklers had been running, yet there was a dry rectangular shape centered in her space. Lori suspected Chad had stayed the night and just left.

Both mornings, Robin and Chad were already gone when Lori entered the house. The townhouse smelled of recently cooked food and dirty dishes were hastily left in the sink.

They were not seen or heard from again until the evening time when Lori was leaving for work. Neither Chad nor Robin spoke to Lori.

Lori decided to leave work an hour early to see if Chad was sneaking and staying overnight with Robin.

Lori's concerns were validated when she pulled in and there was Chad's car in her parking space, covered in dew and water from the sprinklers. It had apparently been there most if not all of the night.

Upon entering the house, Lori heard someone getting into the shower and whispering upstairs. She waited for them to come down.

Robin told her Chad had just gotten there and needed to take a shower.

"Why did he not take a shower at his own house?" Lori asked.

"He just got here to give me a ride to school and didn't have a chance to shower at home," Robin said.

Lori mentioned that his car appeared to have been there all night. She was disappointed that Robin was lying.

"We will be leaving shortly," Robin said.

"Are you was aware of how much debt Chad is in?" Lori asked.

Robin looked perplexed.

"He said he's had some little things," she said, "like needing tires for his car."

Chad came to the top of the stairs and started calling for Robin to come upstairs.

"Robin and I are talking," Lori yelled.

Chad's tone became more demanding. "Robin! I need you now!"

Robin ran upstairs to see what Chad wanted. She did not come back downstairs until he was ready to leave with her.

Lori realized that Robin was not aware of Chad's financial situation.

Lori decided to act. She could see this was a toxic relationship. The only thing she could think of to get Robin out from underneath Chad's control was to send her back home to live at their mother's house. Chad would not be able to sneak sleepovers with Robin there.

Lori called their mom and told her about what had been going on and expressed her concerns. Lori's mother agreed.

Lori waited for the two to arrive back to the townhouse. Lori was hoping to present the news privately to Robin; however, Chad insisted on being a part of it.

"I think you need to move back home with Mom," Lori told Robin. "It would give you the opportunity to save up money. You haven't been able to living with me."

Chad's face started to turn red with anger. His jaw clenched. He started to leave and insisted that Robin go with him.

Robin moved out by the end of the month, back into her mom's home. She didn't speak to Lori during the move, and continued to not speak to her for almost a month after. Lori kept tabs on Robin through their mother; she still had concerns.

Sending Robin back home turned out to be the right decision for her. Robin started to like having some time to herself and started to redecorate her bedroom. Chad was not allowed to stay past 10:00 pm and was not allowed to come over before 8:00 am.

This, of course, made Chad become even more obsessed with Robin. He would leave at 10:00 pm, then drive home and call Robin multiple times, keeping her on the phone into the early morning hours. Their mother made a new rule that Robin could not receive phone calls after 11:00 pm unless it's an emergency or before 8:00 am. Robin was an adult, but she complied because she was living under her mother's roof.

Chad could not handle the new rules. He would call Robin's phone throughout the night, often leaving as many as thirty messages.

Later, Lori found out Chad would show up at Robin's bedroom window, knocking, wanting to know why she was not answering her phone. He would accuse her of having a man with her and would make her get up and turn her bedroom light on so that he could see inside, to prove she was alone. Some of the times the commotion would disturb their mother's sleep; she would get up and tell him to leave and to stop his crazy behavior. She threatened to call the police; Robin pleaded with her not to if Chad promised to leave.

Chad wanted control of every waking moment of Robin's time. In the evenings, Robin worked as a cashier in the local drug store. Chad stayed in the store her entire shift. He would walk around the store and come to the front whenever a male customer approached Robin's register. If Chuck felt the transaction took more time than it should, he would approach Robin to ask what was the customer was talking to her about. He would even do this in front of customers and insist on an answer. He would leave the store at closing time, only to linger in the parking lot to drive Robin home or follow her home.

One day, Robin's manager approached her and told her that Chad could not linger in the store while she was working. When Robin conveyed this to Chad, he began to sit the entire shift in his car in front of the store, watching Robin cashier through the plate glass window.

He would stay her entire shift. Because of that, Chad got fired from his job for repeatedly not showing up or calling in sick.

Robin did not learn that Chad had lost his job until a month later, when his car was repossessed.

He then bought a used motorcycle and continued to spy on Robin from the parking lot whenever she worked. She did not know he was continuing to watch her; he had told her that he was working at a new job.

One day, a customer was checking out and lingered to ask Robin for directions. The customer was a man who was new to the area. He asked Robin for directions to a local pizza place.

While Robin explained to the man how to get to the pizzeria, Chad came rushing into the store. He confronted the man.

"What did you say to her?" Chad demanded. "You're trying to get a date with her!"

The manager overheard the commotion at the front of the store and immediately came to the front.

"I'm going to call the police if you did not leave this store," the manager told Chad. He apologized to the customer.

Robin finished her shift. At the end of it, her manager approached her and expressed his concern about Chad's behavior.

"If it happens again, I'll be forced to fire you," he told her.

Robin was picked up by her mother. On the way home, Chad phoned Robin wanting to know if the man in the store was driving her home.

"My mom picked me up," Robin said. "She's bringing me home."

"Why are you leaving so late?" Chad questioned her.

"The manager detained me," she said. "He told me he'll have to fire me if you show up at the store again."

It was as if Chad did not hear Robin at all. He just continued to question her about the man.

Chad kept Robin on the phone until she arrived home. When she got there, he was in her driveway on his motorcycle, waiting.

After Robin and her mother entered their home, Chad came in, trailing along.

Robin noticed things in her bedroom had been moved and were missing. Chad had let himself in through her bedroom window and gone through her things. He admitted this to Robin after her mom left.

"I needed gas money for my motorcycle," he said. "I took the money from your coin jar."

Robin did not mention his break-in to anyone until later.

Lori called Robin and asked Robin to be her Maid of Honor. Robin was thrilled with the idea until she told Chad about the news, and he would also be in the bridal party as one of the ushers.

"I do not want you walking down the aisle with another man!" Chad told Robin. "I'll only allow you to be in the wedding if you walk with me."

This would make him the best man. The groom was not interested in having Chad be his best man, so he said "no" to that arrangement. Chad then forbade Robin to be Maid of Honor or in the wedding party at all.

Robin was upset. She declined Lori's offer.

The semester ended. Robin finished her classes and was out for the Christmas break. She was looking forward to attending a new college for architecture.

Chad knew this meant Robin would have to attend a college farther away, since those closer to her home would not give her the credits she needed for architecture. He convinced Robin to take a semester off so that they could both work and save up more money for their wedding.

"I want to be married sooner," Chad told Robin. "I want to be married before you leave for school."

Robin considered it; she still needed a car of her own and would need one for school. So she complied and started working full time at the drug store. Chad promised she would finish school after they married.

In the meantime, Chad increased his control and filled up every minute of Robin's time when she was off from work. At Chad's insistence, Robin attended church with him every Sunday even though her Christian faith was different from his. Chad was obligated to attend church every Sunday because his father was the minister, and he refused to let Robin out of his sight.

Robin had her annual doctor's appointment. Chad went along. He gave her permission to write a check from their joint account to cover the cost. Robin had been putting her whole weekly paycheck into the account since moving back in with her mother.

Robin received a call three days later from the doctor's office that her check had been returned due to insufficient funds. Robin was shocked; Chad had deposited her paycheck the day before the appointment. It should have more than covered the cost, not to mention the thousands she herself had already put into the account. She had never made a withdrawal, either. She was saving every penny, and thought Chad was, too.

She thought it was a mistake. Chad always handled the account.

Robin called the bank. She was told the balance of the account was negative seventeen dollars with the insufficient funds charge from her bounced check. In disbelief, Robin checked further and found that her paychecks had been withdrawn or spent within forty-eight hours every time they were deposited and the only deposits that were being made into the account where hers. Not one deposit was made by Chad.

Robin got off the phone with the bank and confronted him. Chad admitted that he had taken the money.

"I needed it to buy my motorcycle," he said, "and pay my bills, since I haven't been working."

Robin felt heartbroken and betrayed.

Chad convinced her that he had every intention of putting the money back in time for their wedding and that his grandfather was going to give him the money.

"I won't make any more purchases from the account without discussing it with you," he promised.

Later that week, Robin was off from work while Chad had something church-related he had to do with his dad. Chad insisted Robin go, too.

"I have a headache," Robin said. "I can't go."

Chad, not trusting Robin, made her promise she would head to his parents' home and rest there.

Robin drove her mom's car to Chad's house. Chad's mother let her in. Robin waited for him in his bedroom and watched TV.

While in Chad's bedroom, she found large bags full of pornographic magazines in his closet. She also found an expensive, recently purchased camera, with the receipt. There was also a packet of recently developed pictures. Robin flipped through them and discovered Chad had apparently been spying on and photographing the next door neighbor, her teenage daughter, and the daughter's friends lying out by their pool. The photos appeared to have been taken from Chad's bedroom window.

Robin felt sickened.

She also found the bank statements that showed Chad had been withdrawing money out of their joint checking account, as well as recent receipts for his pornography collection – the dates on which verified that he was spending her hard-earned money on the pornography, not paying bills or saving money for their wedding, like he had said.

Robin left Chad's house and stopped at Lori's house on the way home. From there she called Chad. She confronted him and ended the relationship.

Robin cried and told Lori about everything that happened. She was terribly angry and hurt. Lori offered for her to stay over with her, but Robin had her mother's car and needed to return home.

"Chad's jealousy scares me at times," Robin said. "I tried to leave him multiple times, but whenever I did, he would threaten to kill himself. And I was afraid he might harm me, too."

Robin was upset, but seemed somewhat relieved at the same time.

After several hours, Robin left to go home. Lori stayed on the phone while she drove home to ensure that she would get home safely.

Chad passed Robin on her way home. It appeared he was heading away from her house. He recognized her and turned around to follow her.

Robin pulled into her driveway and went quickly into the house before Chad could get off his motorcycle. She locked the door. Chad pounded on the door.

"Leave, Chad!" Robin yelled through the door. "Go home!"

Robin's mother was awakened by the commotion.

"Come on, Robin, just let me talk to you," Chad pleaded.

"Leave, or I'll call the police!" Robin threatened.

"The police are on the way," Robin's mother said behind her.

She had not actually called, but Chad left quickly.

Robin told her mother what had happened. In the meantime, Chad continued to call Robin's phone throughout the night and into the early morning hours. He called forty-one times. She had her ringer tuned off while she slept and woke up to all the missed calls and messages filling her inbox. Robin did not respond.

The next day, Robin's mother dropped her off at work. Then her mother went next door to the grocery store. She planned to pick Robin up later that evening at the end of her shift.

Within minutes of Robin getting on her register, Chad showed up, begging her to take him back. He was creating a scene inside the store.

"Please leave," Robin told him.

The manager overheard the commotion and came to Robin's register.

"You both need to leave," he said. "I'm sorry to have to let you go, Robin, but I can't tolerate this behavior any longer. Customers have been complaining."

The manager allowed Robin to wait inside until Chad rode off on his motorcycle.

When he was gone, Robin went next door to find her mother in the grocery store. She told her what had just happened. They finished shopping together and drove back home.

Lori called Robin to check in on her and she told Lori about her job loss. Lori invited her to have a girl's day the next day.

"Lunch is on me," Lori said.

Robin happily agreed.

So the next day, Lori picked her up, and they went shopping and then to lunch. They had a great time.

When they got back to the car, Robin had twenty-seven missed calls from Chad. They had only been gone three hours.

When Lori pulled into Robin's driveway to drop her off, Chad pulled up behind her car. He approached Robin as she got out of the car.

"Were you out on a date?" he asked her.

"No," Lori replied, "she has been with me."

Chad seemed desperate and was breathing heavily.

"Why were you not answering your phone if you weren't on a date?" he asked Robin.

"Please just leave," Lori said, "and stop harassing us. Your behavior has not been okay. You need to get help! You have serious mental issues!"

Robin headed to the front door and went inside. Lori waited outside for Chad to leave and for their mother to arrive home from work so as not to leave Robin home alone.

When Robin entered the house, she went to her bedroom to put away the shoes she had bought. Once again, she could see Chad had broken into her bedroom through the window. This time he had stolen her jewelry, including her engagement ring, and all of the items she had been buying over time for when they would have been married.

Robin phoned to confront him. She agreed not to report him to the police in exchange for Chad to leave her alone.

"No more calls," she told him, "no more pop-in visits, no more driving around my neighborhood, and no more following me. I'll call the police and I'll tell your parents' church about your addiction to pornography. I will never, ever be your girlfriend again!"

He agreed to leave her alone and she hung up.

A month and a half, later Robin found a new job selling Rainbow vacuum cleaners. The schedule was flexible and would work around both her upcoming school schedule and her mother's work schedule, since they were still sharing her mother's car.

Robin went through the training, and within three weeks had sold two of the $2500 vacuums. This paid a good commission to her. She was happy.

Robin started talking to a male friend she knew from school and considered going to the movies with him as friends. She was not quite ready yet for anything more, but thought getting out and seeing a movie with a friend would not be so bad.

The very next day, Robin arrived at her work for the morning meeting and territory assignment to sell vacuums. To her surprise, Chad was introduced in the meeting as a new employee salesperson.

This concerned Robin.

Chad approached her.

"I've moved on," he said. "I want us to be friends."

"I can be your friend," Robin said, "but I need to make it clear I am not to be considered your girlfriend."

Chad nodded his head.

The morning was filled with yet another surprise when Robin found out that Chad would be coming along with her and a seasoned salesperson for training. Robin, still feeling a bit uneasy, decided to give Chad the benefit of the doubt and not say anything to the supervisor about her troubled past with him.

So they started working and training together.

On Wednesday, the supervisor training them was unable to go along on their sales route. He encouraged Robin and Chad to go out together, just the two of them.

Robin thought about it. She decided since she was the one driving her mother's car, she could leave Chad behind if he made her feel uncomfortable, so she agreed.

The day went well.

This continued for the rest of the week.

The following week, Robin had to call out of work one day because her mother's car was going to be serviced. She had no way to get to work or go out into the community and sell vacuums. The manager called Robin and offered to pick her up and bring her to work.

"That would be okay," Robin said, and they hung up. Robin got dressed and packed a lunch to take with her.

When Chad arrived at work, he asked where Robin was.

"I'm about ready to leave to go and pick her up," the manager said.

"I can pick her up," Chad volunteered.

The manager agreed to let him, a decision he would soon regret.

The manager gave Chad the keys to his car since Chad still only had a motorcycle. Chad drove over to Robin's house and pulled in the driveway. Robin came outside, locking the door behind her, and headed to the car, expecting to see the manager.

According to a neighbor, Robin appeared hesitant about getting into the car. It seemed the person driving the car had to coax her to get in. She finally did.

Robin never made it to work.

Chad took Robin back to his house with the manager's car. His parents were not home. Chad's father, a Baptist minister, and his mother, a second-grade schoolteacher, were respectively at the Baptist church and private school just a few blocks away, working.

It is unknown what happened between 9:30 am, when Chad picked Robin up, and 11:30 am, when Chad made the phone call to his father.

He called his father first, not 911. Chad's father was at the Board of Members meeting that day when he received the call from Chad about an incident that had occurred in his home.

"Get off the phone and dial 911" Chad's father told him. "I'll be on my way."

As Chad's father left the meeting, he asked one board member, who was also an attorney, to come with him.

When Chad's father pulled up in front of his house, the ambulance had just pulled in ahead of them. The police pulled in behind him while Chad's father and the attorney got out of the car.

The paramedics prepared Robin for transport. She was still alive but unresponsive.

The police started to question Chad. He told them that he had left with his manager's car to get food for him and Robin to eat, and when he returned, just as he opened the front door, he saw her standing in the family room ahead of him and heard the gun go off.

The attorney interrupted the policeman. "Excuse me. I am this young man's attorney."

This greatly hindered the investigation, since Chad was the only witness, and the last person with Robin. Because of Chad's attorney being onsite, neither Chad nor his father had to tell anyone what Robin's name was. She was referenced and flown to the trauma center as Jane Doe.

At around 11:30 am that day, thoughts of Robin came to Lori's mind. Lori had an ominous feeling and could not get Robin off her mind.

Lori called her to see how she was doing and got her voicemail. Lori left Robin a message asking her to call her back. When Lori hung up, she hoped that Robin would call back soon.

The afternoon progressed, and at 2:30 pm, Lori's husband, Jared, left for work as a Deputy Sheriff for the county. He had just changed rotation at the Sheriff's Department to the evening shift and worked from 3:00 pm to 11:00 pm.

At around 6:30 pm, Jared came home early. Lori was surprised to see him. She jumped up to greet him at the door.

"Are you home for dinner?" Lori asked.

"You need to sit down," he responded.

Baffled, Lori asked, "Why?"

"I have some bad news. Please sit down."

By the look on his face, Lori could tell something was very wrong.

"Did you get fired?" she asked.

"No."

"I'm not sitting down," Lori said, "please just tell me?"

He hesitated.

Lori insisted. "What happened?"

"There has been a death in your family," he said. "I'm still trying to get the details."

Lori was in shock and disbelief.

"Oh no!" she said, finally. "Was it Ryan?"

Lori assumed that it was her older brother, Ryan, since he had previously had some issues with drugs, alcohol, and a risky way of life. She thought it had to be him.

Lori started to cry. She asked questions about what happened, but before Jared could answer her, the phone rang.

Jared answered it.

Lori overheard him saying, "...in Palm Springs this morning."

Lori's mind raced.

"Oh my God," she thought, "my brother must have been in a bad car accident."

Her heart raced and squeezed. Lori felt sick.

"What happened," she asked Jared, "was there a car accident?"

He was still on the phone, unable to answer her, and continued speaking with the person on the phone. Lori overheard him say, "Rainbow vacuum cleaners."

Her body went numb with shock. Breathing became painful.

"No, no," Lori thought, "not my baby sister, not my baby sister who just turned twenty. Robin works for Rainbow Vacuums."

Then Lori blurted out, "Rainbow Vacuums? My sister Robin sells Rainbow vacuums!"

In total disbelief, Lori asked, "Was Robin with my brother, too?"

She did not remember sitting down. Her Thoughts were racing through her mind as she tried to make sense of what she was hearing. She prayed that there was somehow a mistake! She prayed that both her brother and sister were okay.

Jared got off the phone.

He turned to Lori and said, "It's Robin."

"ROBIN!" Lori screamed through her tears. "Robin! My baby sister is dead! No, it can't be!" Lori sobbed. "I just spoke with her the other day. I just called her today. She's supposed to call me back."

Lori picked up her phone and dialed Robin's number. She got her voicemail again. When Lori heard Robin's recorded voice, she sobbed loudly. "Not Robin!"

Lori looked up at Jared. "Are they sure it was my family's Robin?"

Jared nodded. "Yes."

Lori fell back onto the sofa. Crying, she asked, "Oh dear God, beautiful Robin, what happened?"

Before Jared could answer, Lori blurted out multiple questions. "Where is she now? Does my mother know yet? Does anybody know besides me?"

Lori had never felt so much emotional pain in her life. It felt like a semi-truck was sitting on her stomach and chest. She could hardly breathe.

"Oh my God! OH MY GOD! NO! Not my baby sister!" she screamed.

Jared told Lori that his father, who was a detective with the county, shared an office with a brand-new detective. The new detective was the one that investigated the scene. However, since an attorney was also on the scene, representing Chad, they were not able to get the victim's name or any information on her identity.

"Your family has not been notified," Jared said, "because the dead girl could not be identified."

By coincidence, the new detective asked the assistance of Jared's father to help locate the family of this deceased girl with no name. The new detective showed Jared's father the photos of the scene. Jared's father immediately recognized the girl in the photos.

"That is my daughter-in-law's sister, Robin," he told the detective.

Before notifying the family, Jared's father called Jared and asked that he come to the office to positively identify and confirm his belief. Jared confirmed that his father was correct. It was Robin.

Robin was fatally shot sometime between 10:00 am and 11:30 am in Chad's home. She was shot with a 357-magnum at close range. The gun was owned by Chad's father and was kept on the top shelf inside the minister's master bedroom closet. The bullet entry wound was on the left side of Robin's head, about an inch behind her ear. The bullet trajectory went upward and exited at the top right side of her head, above her right ear. The whole back of Robin's head was gone. The bullet had missed the brain centers responsible for breathing; therefore, Robin was still alive when the police arrived on the scene.

No one knows how long Robin was actually left lying on Chad's floor before he finally called his dad. Robin was loaded into an ambulance and transported to the Trauma Hawk helicopter that was waiting in the church parking lot, minutes from Chad's house. Robin, as Jane Doe, was flown to the hospital. She went into cardiac arrest four times while in flight and was resuscitated. They landed on the hospital helipad and ushered her into the emergency room. A team of doctors and medical staff converged, trying to save Jane Doe's life. After about forty minutes, she was pronounced dead in the emergency room.

"She was taken to the morgue," Jared said, "then picked up by the coroner's office for autopsy."

Chad was in custody.

In disbelief, Lori uttered, "Why would he want to hurt Robin? Oh my God, he finally got her!"

Then a flood of questions came to mind.

"How did she end up at Chad's house to begin with?" Lori sobbed.

"The case is under investigation," Jared replied. "Chad had an attorney onsite to represent him, which made it hard to question him or even get Robin's name." He assured Lori he would update her as he found out new information.

"I want to see Robin!" Lori blurted out.

"Robin's body was taken to the coroner's office for autopsy," Jared said. "They won't release her until the autopsy is finished."

Lori sobbed in grief. Then the thought hit her that her family still did not know about Robin.

Lori knew that her mother was at work. She cared for an elderly lady in the evenings. Lori called one of her mother's coworkers, Bea, and asked for her help. Lori gave her brief details about Robin and asked if she would meet her at her mother's work.

"I need you to cover the rest of my mother's shift."

Bea agreed and would meet Lori at her mother's workplace.

Lori got into the back of Jared's police car. While heading down Interstate 95 to her mom's work, Lori called her brother, Ryan, but could not reach him. She left a message for him to call her back right away.

Lori then called her other sister, Lisa, and told her what had happened. Lisa was devastated and in disbelief.

Just then, the beep came through from the other line. It was her brother's wife, Payton. Lori hung up with her sister to tell Payton about the tragedy. Then Lori received a distraught call back from Ryan.

Ryan and Payton's home was directly behind Lori's mother's house.

"Does our mother know yet?" Ryan asked.

Lori told him that she was on her way to their mother's work to pick her up and tell her. Ryan offered to contact their father and let him know. Lori agreed.

"You and Payton meet us at Mom's house in about thirty minutes," Lori said. Then she phoned her sister Mary. Mary planned to call their brother Richard.

On the way to tell Lori's mother, Jared drove past the cemetery near her mother's work. Lori reflected that she and Robin had passed through the same cemetery just a few weeks earlier.

"We were taking a short cut to my workplace to get my paycheck," Lori told Jared. "I had made mention to Robin that if something ever happened to me, and I died, that I wanted her to do my makeup, because she is the only one that knew how I applied it. Robin then responded, 'Me too, I want you to do mine also, and I want a white casket with a huge spray of daisies.' Then I said, 'Let's stop talking about this, it's too creepy,' and we changed the subject.

"We talked about Robin's break up with Chad and many of the things she never told anyone that he did. She spoke of one time when she arrived home with our mother. They were startled by Chad's presence in Robin's bedroom. He had parked his motorcycle around the corner where they would not see it. Robin said that he had come in through her bedroom window. Chad thought that Robin was home and just not answering the door to him or his calls. I asked her if anyone called the police and she said no. I insisted that they still call the police and report it."

Lori had been concerned about Chad's behavior, that he had called Robin's phone so many times in the short time they were out together shopping.

Robin had rationalized it and said, "He will not do it again."

She had said that she got him to leave her house and that he had not come back to her house since.

"Yet he drives by your house and still calls excessive times a day," Lori had pointed out.

"I again expressed my concern," Lori said to Jared, "and told her that she could come stay at my house if she ever felt the need. Robin felt that everything would be alright, and she decided not to. She had just started her new job selling vacuums."

Then reality brought Lori back in thought to the present.

"He got her! He killed her!" she said loudly. "Why didn't Robin and my mother call the police? I should have called the police!"

Lori still felt numb and in shock.

They pulled up in front of her mother's work. Bea was standing outside in the parking lot waiting for them to arrive. Jared left the car running in the street.

"She doesn't know I'm here," Bea whispered.

Lori went to the door and her mother greeted them. She had seen the police car pull up from the window.

"Hi, Lori," her mom said, "you are not working tonight?"

Lori told her that Bea was there to relieve her.

"You need to gather your things and come with us."

Bewildered, her mother asked, "Is everything okay?"

"Something bad happened," Lori said. "I'll tell you in the car."

But her mother wanted to know. As they walked to the car, she asked, "Is someone dead?"

"Get in the car first," Lori said, "and then I will tell you."

As they got into the car, Lori's mother asked, "Is it your brother?"

"No," Lori told her. "It's Robin."

She gasped and said, "My Rob!"

She clutched her heart and sobbed.

"Our Robin?" she asked.

"Yes," Lori replied.

"I left Robin at home this morning," Lori's mom said in disbelief. "I knocked on her bedroom door to tell her that I was leaving and that I loved her. She said, 'I love you, too, Mom.' She didn't even have a car to go anywhere today. How could this happen? Was it an accident?"

Lori told her that Robin was shot in the back of her head and that Chad was in police custody.

"Not my Rob, little Robbie," Lori's mother cried. "Oh, Lori, he did it, if he could not have her, he didn't want anyone else to, either.

"Where did Chad even get a gun?"

While driving, Jared explained that the gun belonged to Chad's father. Both Lori and her mother exclaimed simultaneously, "How did she end up at Chad's house?"

"Robin stayed home from work today because she had no car," Lori's mom said. "It had to be dropped it off for service." She was still in disbelief. "I knocked on Robin's bedroom door this morning to say 'goodbye.' Robin sounded a little under the weather." She sobbed. "Oh, I cannot believe it! My beautiful Robin is dead."

As they pulled into the driveway of Lori's mother and Robin's home, Ryan and his wife were waiting in the yard. Ryan came over to the car and hugged both Lori and their mother as they got out of the car while all four of them cried. He immediately started asking questions about what had happened. Jared informed Ryan of what was known so far.

While inside Lori's mother's house, Lori went into Robin's bedroom. She sat down on her bed. She picked up her pillow hugged and smelled her scent on it. She started talking out loud to God in her room, expressing her thoughts of disbelief and asking for clues to what happened.

Jared heard back from a call with the detective and informed the family that Chad was sticking to his story that Robin committed suicide, but there was limited proof for that.

"It is still being investigated due to major inconsistencies with Chad's claims compared to the only evidence they could get from the scene and Robin's body," Jared said. "For one, Robin was right-handed and the entry wound was on her left side. Chad was left-handed. The trajectory of the 357-magnum indicated it could have been from someone behind Robin shooting the gun. There was no suicide note. It appeared the two had been arguing prior to the gun shot, as pornographic magazines and Robin's engagement ring that had been stolen previously by Chad were tossed into the corner of the room. Because of the attorney being on the scene, Chad was never checked for gun residue. The fingerprints on the gun were from Robin's left hand. If Robin had shot that powerful gun with one hand, it would have been with her right hand. That powerful gun, for a little lady to be shooting with her non-dominant hand, even with two hands, because of the recoil on it, would be hard to hit the target for someone like Robin – especially in a contorted position, which she would have had to have been in to match up with the trajectory of the bullet's path."

None of Robin's family believed Chad's story.

While sitting on Robin's bed, Lori had an overwhelming feeling of, "Why are you in my room?"

Lori could see rippling in the air next to her, like gasoline vapors. She turned her head and thought she saw Robin standing in front of her.

Lori gasped, and then asked, "Robin, what happened?"

"Get out of my room!" Robin said. "Why are you going through my things?" Robin's spirit motioned for Lori to leave.

It was clear to Lori that she was violating Robin's privacy.

Because her death was sudden, Robin did not seem to know that she was dead.

"You're dead," Lori told Robin.

A look of dismay and confusion came over Robin's face. She faded from sight.

Lori could no longer see Robin's form, but she could feel Robin's disbelief and could still see rippling in the air. Lori continued to speak out loud into Robin's bedroom and asked her to go to the light.

"A relative will be there to help you cross over," she told Robin's spirit. Then Lori prayed for a loved one from the other side to come and help Robin.

Lori got up and started to look for clues. Robin's things were left in a way that appeared as if she had planned on returning. She obviously planned to take the ride to work; she had packed herself a lunch that she had forgotten and was left behind in the refrigerator.

When it came time to leave, Lori stopped at the door to hug and kiss her mother goodbye. Out of her peripheral vision, to her mother's right, she caught a glimpse of Robin standing right next to her mother with her arms out, gesturing for a hug. It caught Lori by surprise. She looked directly at the spot where she had seen Robin standing in her peripherals and there was nothing there. She knew in that moment that this was such a sudden and unexpected tragedy that even Robin's soul was not prepared. She was stuck in between dimensions and still earthbound. Her soul was still trying to make sense of what had happened and was not ready to be dead.

Jared and Lori headed home. On the way home, Lori told Jared what she had seen and about the feelings she experienced in Robin's room.

"Now it makes sense," Lori told Jared. "She was there the whole time."

Suddenly, Lori said, "We need to go back to my mother's house so that I can hug Robin. I felt her disappointment when I walked right past her as if she were not there and ignored her gesture to hug."

Jared started to turn around. Then Lori changed her mind and decided to go home, as she felt that she had been the only one to see her and that could create some discord for other family members.

They arrived home and got ready for bed. Lori prayed to God to help Robin cross over. She asked to have one of their relatives come and help her find her way because her soul seemed confused.

They awoke the next morning and went back to Lori's mother's house to help plan for Robin's funeral. Robin's body was being released from the coroner's office and they needed to know what funeral home to send it to. Everyone was still in great disbelief and shock.

As they all started to gather, Lori told her mother about seeing Robin in the house the night before, standing right next to her as she and Jared were leaving.

Ryan showed up at their mother's home. He was anxious to tell everyone what had occurred in the early morning hours.

"I was lying in bed in a sort of twilight sleep," he said. He was aware of his surroundings, yet not quite ready to open his eyes. "As I lay in bed, the room filled with light, and our sister, Robin, stood at my bedside, along with my great grandmother, Ida, and a man who seemed familiar, but I could not place. Robin stood there smiling. So did our great grandmother. I asked Robin questions about what had happened, and she would not speak. She just smiled. It was as if she was behind a glass wall.

"The man reached his hand out to me, and we touched hands, and when this happened, the room burst with even brighter light and tingling went up my arm and through my body."

Ryan said he knew in that moment that the male spirit guide was the one who watched over him personally and guided Ryan with his talents.

"The light was so bright," Ryan said, "yet easy on the eyes. And then they were gone."

Ryan felt that Robin wanted everyone to know that she was okay, that she had crossed over, and that she was with loved ones on the other side.

The family sat down at Lori's mother's dining room table to plan for Robin's burial and funeral. They started with the yellow pages to find a local funeral home. Lori let everyone know what Robin had said about her end of life wishes.

They spoke to Lori's older sisters, Mary and Lisa, on the phone and updated them on what they had found out. Mary and Lisa kept the rest of the rest of the family up to date. They also felt strongly that Chad had murdered Robin.

Most of the day was a blur.

That night, when Jared and Lori went home and finally got into bed, Lori did not even remember falling asleep; nonetheless, she was awakened in the night by Jared saying he had just seen Robin standing at the foot of their bed.

"She was with someone and seemed safe," Jared said.

Lori started to cry. She wanted to see her, too. She could smell her perfume lingering in the room.

When Lori phoned my mother that morning, her mother told her Robin had visited her bedside in the early morning hours, also.

"I was lying in my bed and smelled Robin's perfume," her mother said. "When I opened my eyes, Robin was standing with Great Grandma Ida next to my bed."

Lori's mother said she had started to cry and inquired what happened, but they just smiled and faded away. She could feel much love coming from both spirits.

Lori's mother arose that morning and went to the bathroom to turn the water on for her bath. She added some bubbles and left to get a towel out of the hallway closet.

When she returned to shut the water off, she found one of Robin's long dark hairs gently laid, full length, on top of the bubbles in the tub.

This happened again on the day of Robin's funeral, and many other times since. It was Robin's way of communicating with her mother from the other side.

A Word from the Author

Normally I would stop this chapter here, since I have covered the experience of sudden death. However, even though this part of the chapter does not show the effects of sudden death versus natural death versus near death, some curious minds might want to know how the rest of Robin's story played out. This is what happened.

The family decided on a funeral home and notified the coroner's office where to release Robin's body. Lori and her mother went to the funeral home to sign papers. While there, Robin's body arrived from the coroner's office.

Lori asked to see Robin. The mortician discouraged it until after the body was processed and readied for viewing. Lori insisted.

The mortician again recommended not seeing her until the viewing due to her head and autopsy wounds, but Lori continued to insist.

"I want to see her, too," said Robin's mother.

So the mortician had Robin's body arranged in a way that they would be able to view her.

The mortician told them Robin was ready. Then he led them to a room where Robin's body laid on a stretcher.

She was beautiful, a sleeping angel. Lori touched Robin's hand; her skin was cold but still very soft and smooth. Lori held Robin's hand, trying to warm it with her own hands.

Robin's mother sobbed, "My Robbie!"

Lori leaned forward and kissed Robin's cheek. She looked like herself only sleeping peacefully, and her cheek was smooth and soft.

"I am thankful that I insisted to see her before they embalmed her," Lori said. Then she said her final goodbye to Robin.

Lori and her mother headed for the doorway, looking back several times to say goodbye and tell Robin they loved her.

They both agreed that they were happy that they got to see Robin and have that private moment with her.

They went back to the previous room with the mortician and planned for the viewing and funeral. Lori told the mortician about her promise to Robin. "I told her if something ever happened to her, that I would do her makeup."

The following day, Lori went with her best friend to the funeral home to do just that.

Lori was shocked at how the embalming fluid made Robin look bloated, like she was fifty pounds heavier than she was, and how her skin was hard and gritty. Robin's hair had also been cut in front. Lori reflected on the day before, getting to kiss Robin's soft smooth cheek, and again was so thankful she had. This body hardly resembled her beautiful sister.

While applying Robin's makeup, Lori kept catching glimpses out of her peripheral vision of Robin's spirit standing nearby.

At one point, Lori turned to her left and asked Robin's spirit what happened. Robin would just continue to smile and fade away.

When Lori finished putting on Robin's makeup, it was time to go home and get ready for the viewing. The viewing was scheduled that evening.

When Lori's family arrived at the funeral home for the viewing, they had hoped to be ahead of everyone else, since the viewing didn't start for thirty more minutes. They wanted a private moment with Robin, and family that had flown in had not seen her yet.

The moment was tainted when they found Chad had already gotten there first, with his parents. His family had taken the liberty of attaching a rose to Robin's casket lid. Robin's family was shocked to even see Chad there, since the incident was still under investigation and he was a suspect.

Chad, who claimed Robin committed suicide in front of him, was released due to lack of enough evidence. He never spent one night in jail and had been home with his family. The investigation did not go further than a suicide. The whole investigation was not thoroughly completed due to the presence of Chad's attorney on the scene, and perhaps the detective being new and not as experienced.

Everything that was brought to the police's attention was not followed up on. The police said it was listed as an accidental death since there was not enough evidence for a suicide. However, when the death certificate came back, it was based on the coroner's report, and it was listed as a suicide.

Robin died in the early 1990s, before stalking was taken seriously. The interview with her family before and after Robin's death about all the bizarre behavior from Chad towards Robin fell on deaf ears. They felt nothing they said was even being taken into consideration. Plus, Chad was a citizen with no prior record and had a whole church to back up how wonderful he was.

The bullet entry was on the left side and Robin was right-handed. Chad was left-handed. The angle of the bullet trajectory would have been impossible for Robin to have accomplished unless she was a contortionist. The gun was a 357-magnum, a powerful gun to be held with one hand, and a non-dominant one, at that. It would have been near impossible for her to have done it.

There was no suicide note. Her packed lunch for that day had been forgotten in the refrigerator at her mom's house.

Nobody seemed to question why Chad had not taken Robin to work, knowing the manager was waiting for his car to be returned, or why Chad decided to take Robin to his house.

No one asked why Chad kept the manager's car for hours and drove it to go get food for him and Robin to eat, leaving Robin at his house. Why didn't he take her with him to get food then continue onto work like he was supposed to hours before?

Chad was not checked for gun powder residue until ten days later. The parents' bedroom where the gun was supposedly retrieved from was never dusted for prints to determine who actually took the gun from the closet. No one seemed to think it was odd that the only fingerprints on the gun were Robin's. This gun belonged to Chad's father, who would have handled it at some point, leaving at least his prints. Why weren't any of his prints on the gun? How did Robin's stolen engagement ring end up at Chad's house?

Chad stood in the chapel of the funeral home at the front of the room, with his parents, near the casket. It was as if Chad expected for people to give their condolences to him.

Chad did not shed one tear, nor did he approach Robin's family to say anything. He just stood there until a few of his friends arrived. Then he went out to the parking lot and was seen by multiple people joking and laughing with his friends.

The same happened the next day at the burial site. Chad picked up Robin's last paycheck from Rainbow Vacuum claiming he was going to bring it to Robin's family. He instead deposited it into the joint checking account he and Robin had shared and took the money. The police were told about this, too.

When Chad was confronted with this, his father answered for Chad and stated that Robin owed Chad the money.

Chad was seen by several people in a disco two weeks after Robin was buried, dancing with an older woman whom it was said he married approximately ten weeks later.

The incident supposedly occurred at around 11:00 am. Due to Chad's lack of cooperation, and having a very new detective on the scene, many things were not done. Robin went alone to the hospital and family was not notified until close to 7:00 pm. Robin's body was already at the coroner's office. The whole investigation was never completed properly because of Chad's attorney being onsite. Even though the police suspected foul play, they could not question the only other witness, because she was dead. Chad got off free.

Chapter 6

To Cross Over or Not to Cross Over

In the previous chapter, some things were mentioned more than once in reference to crossing over or choosing not to. Before the details of death unfold, here are some things everyone should know.

When a soul transitions into death, they do not have to cross over. They can choose to remain earthbound. When they choose to stay earthbound, this creates issues that are not so good on many levels. They eventually become ghosts and lost souls until they are either assisted over by the living or are finally absorbed into the gray space of the dimensions.

Since the time frame on the other side is different than ours, that absorption could take centuries. That is why there seems to be somewhat of a buildup of sightings and hauntings during our current time frame.

Most souls joyously choose to cross over. Our earthly dimension is number three. Heaven/home is number five. When a person chooses to cross over, they are assisted past the fourth dimension into the fifth, and from there beyond. In the cases that a soul chooses not to cross over at the time of taking their last physical breath, they become stuck in the fourth dimension, which is a dimension that is not totally earthbound and outside of heaven.

The fourth dimension is used frequently by other realities, as well as lost souls. Other realities appear as they would on the plane from which they came. Ghosts and wandering lost souls appear as they looked at their exit from embodiment. They show up in the clothes they were buried in or died in. It is an area in which a soul can also be on earth without a body. The perception of the lost souls who live there is like swimming underwater without a mask with one's eyes open. Some ghastly things also reside there. Therefore, they prefer to linger in the third dimension most of the time.

Since they have not crossed over, they still present with the cause of death showing such as decapitation, burns, wounds, and cancer. Cancer appears like baby Swiss cheese in the area affected. They still share emotions, addictions, and behaviors that they had when they were fully embodied.

The fourth dimension is not a good place to be, especially for a human soul. That is why they look for shelter in people's homes. Once in someone's home, the negative draw of the lost soul can cause disturbed sleep, exacerbated illnesses, and addictive behaviors.

It is not good idea to have a lost soul lingering in one's home, regardless of whether they appear harmless or not. The lost souls in one's home also invite other entities in that may not be friendly. The negative energy invites other negative energy. Find a way to get them out of your home.

Visits from our loved ones who have crossed over are a good thing. They come and go and do not linger. Lost souls are strangers who linger.

Some souls choose to remain earthbound because of what they felt was their duty to a loved one, in the case of a caretaker who has passed before the person or pet they cared for. When souls do not cross over, they still carry the emotions felt while in body. Their addictions remain. They do not suffer from pain or physical discomfort, but unlike those who have crossed over, the cause of their death remains visible.

Dapper Dan

One evening, I was working my shift and standing with my medication cart outside of a client's room that was in the final stages of transitioning. I have noticed throughout my career that when someone is actively passing, the act draws spectators, both alive and dead. This particular evening, a gentleman appeared, peering around the backside of a pillar. I hesitated to see if he was just passing through.

He appeared to be lingering. So I said, "Hello."

The ghost looked over each of his shoulders to see who I was talking to, assuming it could not be him.

"Hello," I said again, "you there, the gent behind the pillar."

He came from around the pillar and stood next to it, pointing his finger to his chest in a 'who, me?' gesture.

"Yes, you there," I said, "why haven't you crossed over yet?"

Curiously, Dapper Dan approached the medication cart and asked in a heavy Irish brogue, "M'lady, are you able to see me?"

"Of course," I replied, and asked again, "Why have you not crossed over? I have a client who is passing. If you want to cross over, I could help you out."

Dapper Dan was a very handsome fellow who appeared to be in his mid-thirties, and by his clothes, from the early 1800s, complete with a cravat and vest.

I could see that the cause of Dapper Dan's death was present. He had a saucer-sized Swiss cheese blotch on his abdomen area, in the mid-to-upper-right quadrant. When I see this, it usually indicates that the lost soul died from a sort of corrosive disease, like cancer or cirrhosis of the liver.

I asked him again if he wanted to cross over.

"M'lady, I can't cross over," he said.

"Well, of course you can," I replied.

He shook his head. "I cannot cross over because my wife and mistress are on the other side and neither knew about the other."

I couldn't help but smile a bit. This poor guy had been stuck there all this time, because he was afraid of facing the music about his infidelity.

"Well, I am sure they know now!" I told him. I explained that when people cross over, they have a better understanding and ability to forgive.

"Negative earthly emotions do not carry over after one life review," I said. "They may not even be there anymore. And I am sure, at this point, they don't care."

He smiled.

I asked him again if I could help him, and reminded him that not many people could see him.

"And if they could," I continued, "most would run off screaming after seeing a ghost." I stressed the fact that this offer may not ever come again, so he might consider taking it.

He smiled and tilted head in an appreciative gesture then faded away. I never saw him again.

Worry and guilt souls experience during life can keep them here. Religious beliefs and addiction can keep them earthbound, as well. I've seen spirits who have lingered to watch over an ailing loved one whom they expected to die before they did. When the ailing loved one dies and crosses over, the lingering soul gets stuck earthbound.

Shirley

I once had a patient named Shirley. She was a beautiful woman. She and her husband had never had any children. Her only regular visitor was her husband, who often would not be able to come and see her due to his own ailments. I made a point to stop in and visit her while on my shift working as a nurse. She was a highly educated and kind person. She had been diagnosed with terminal cancer.

As she progressed through the stages of decline, she started to talk about the spirits who would come into her room periodically.

I was working the night shift. Shirley had turned her call light on and asked for her pain medication. I gathered her pain pill and proceeded down the long hallway to her room.

About halfway down the hallway, I felt this sensation of someone rushing up on me from behind. I turned around quickly, expecting it to be a staff member, and to my surprise, no one was there.

I was positive someone had come up behind me. It had felt like a male energy.

As I continued down the hallway to Shirley's room, it still seemed as if I was being followed very closely. When I entered Shirley's room, I left the door slightly open for some light from the hallway and left the room light off.

"Who's your friend?" Shirley asked me.

"What do you mean?" I replied.

"The man behind you," Shirley said. "He came in the room with you."

I turned around to look, expecting to see one of the CNAs.

No one was there.

"He's a very busy fellow, isn't he?" Shirley said, and she said 'hello' to him.

"I guess he had something else to do," she continued. "He just walked out of the room."

At the same that Shirley said that, the feeling I was having of being followed closely had instantly subsided. I could feel that he had exited the room.

I asked Shirley what he looked like.

"He was dead, wasn't he?" she said. Then she changed the subject and took her medication.

As I exited Shirley's room, I saw the lost soul in the hallway pacing and somewhat frantic.

"Are you alright?" I asked him.

"I can't find my dog," he said.

I looked at his face and recognized him as one of our dependent clients, but I could not remember his name or where exactly his home was. I knew he was not on the skilled unit. I tried to ask his name, but he vanished down the hallway.

I went to the nurse's station and got out a book of the residences in the dependent and assisted living unit's photo identification book and started looking for the man's photo.

I wanted to do a well check on him. I didn't know how I was going to explain calling security to go with me to wake this man up in the middle of the night, but at the very least I was going to call. I figured I could explain the call by asking him to check his pendant and reset it. Then I would apologize profusely for waking him up.

I never got to make that call.

About twenty-five minutes later, as I diligently looked through the identification books for his photo while managing my client calls, a pendant light went off in one of the villas. I called security to rush me to the call.

A woman who seemed somewhat confused was waiting at the door and said her husband had fallen out of bed and was lying on the carpet next to the bed.

"He had been making gurgling sounds," she said, "and it took me a while to find the cough syrup to give him. Now he's fallen out of bed, and I can't get him to wake up to take the medicine."

The security guard and I went into the bedroom. From the doorway, I could see the man's feet.

The color of his feet indicated to me he was dead. I asked the wife if he had a 'do not resuscitate order' and she didn't know, so I had security call 911 as I positioned myself over the body to initiate CPR. It was obvious he had been gone for hours. His body was cold and had begun to stiffen.

As I affixed a mouthpiece over his nose and mouth, I recognized the man as the one I had been looking for in the identification books.

The paramedics arrived, took over the CPR, and then pronounced him as dead. After helping the wife call her family to notify them of the death and have someone come and stay with her, I noticed a dog bed near the recliner in the living room. I asked about the dog, and she said the dog had to be put to sleep a few days before.

Addiction

If only people on their cigarette break or at the bar for happy hour could see all of the decaying dead corpses hovering around them, trying to get as close as they can to the cigarette smoke or vapors from the alcohol, most people would not be able to get out of that establishment fast enough. They would probably run off screaming, perhaps with soiled garments, never to return.

It is a mind-blowing experience for sure. They still have their senses to sniff and reminisce. They huddle close to the patron and are usually very content remaining earthbound.

I was in a restaurant/bar in Florida. As my friends and I passed the bar to be seated at a table, there were corpses standing huddled around this couple who were having drinks at the bar. The woman was also smoking. One of the decaying corpses had no head – he had placed his head upon the bar right next to this guy's drink. Take that vision to an AA meeting. I am sure it would help many overcome and never touch again.

It is so important to get these types of habits under control before someone crosses over. We enter life clean and free of addiction. It is important to exit the same way. This does not mean that a person with an addiction will not cross over; it's just that they might be more apt to refuse crossing over.

To the soul that is earthbound, regardless of how many times the landscape has been changed over the centuries, the lost soul will still see it as the same as it was during the time they lived. This is the reason oftentimes ghosts are seen doing the same actions over and over, the way they did when they were alive. Like imprints caught in time. They often stay anchored to the same area until released. This is the reason why even brand new homes can have ghostly activity; it's not the age of the house, it's about the ground it is built on. No one knows for sure what was there three hundred years ago. The house could be built on sacred burial or ritualistic native ground.

Lost souls have the same temperament they did when they lived on earth. Some chose not to cross over in order to avoid having their life review. It's not a good place to be, as all types of lost souls, both good and bad, live in the fourth dimension. The earthbound souls have the ability to see and hear both people who are alive and dead, and some of them may appear gruesome.

Chapter 7

Visitations

There are times that souls stop in shortly after death to visit. They want to let their friends and loved ones know they made it over and are okay, especially if they had not been able to see them in person before crossing. There are also times when a soul who is waiting to come in may make their presence known.

John

Growing up, my siblings and I all had gifts. One time, when I was five years old, my brother Ryan, age seven, and I were in our parents' master bedroom. Ryan was playing with his cars on the floor while I dolled myself up with the jewelry from Mom's jewelry box. I was feeling very beautiful and turned to show off my elegance to my brother.

When I turned around, he was sitting frozen and peering into the corner of the room. I looked to see what he was staring at.

A misting was building up in the corner. As the mist thickened, it started to thin in the middle... then we both saw

Ryan's best friend, John, and his entire family standing behind John in the opening. We sat looking at them. John was standing in front of his mother, father, and two siblings, and they were all smiling at Ryan. Then they disappeared, and so did the mist.

Ryan and I ran out of the room in different directions, looking for our mother. Ryan found her first. He told her to come quickly, and that John and his family were in her bedroom.

"Did you let them in?" our mother asked Ryan.

"No," Ryan replied.

"Who did and what are they doing in my bedroom?" she asked.

Our mother walked quickly to greet John's family and get them out of her bedroom.

When no one was there, she became upset, thinking it was a joke Ryan was playing on her.

Ryan explained what he saw. Our mother did not believe him and chastised him for making up such a story. I feared my mother's anger and stayed quiet, lingering in the doorway of the bedroom. Ryan insisted that he was telling the truth, but Mom still threatened to spank him for lying.

Ryan was in the second grade and John was a classmate of his. Ryan knew that John's family had gone on a trip during spring break, and he was anxious for their return. He missed his friend.

On the first day back to school, Ryan went to school looking for his best buddy on the bus. He was not there, and neither were any of John's siblings. When Ryan arrived at school, John was not there, either.

Once the students were situated in their seats, the teacher announced that John would not be coming back to class. He and his entire family had been in a car accident the day before on their way home and were in heaven.

Ryan was heartbroken.

When he returned from school, our mother had already heard about the tragedy. She was speechless. Nothing was mentioned about the visitation the day before. The ability to talk about seeing spirits was not tolerated by my parents. My mother especially found it embarrassing and did not want anyone to find out.

During this era, only crazy people would speak of such things. If word got out into the neighborhood, my family would be labeled with a stigma of having mental illness. We would be shunned and avoided. My father mostly stayed quiet on the subject; I would come to find out later in life, he was the reason we had our gifts.

Jerry

There was a younger man named Jerry in the facility. He was the nephew of one of our members and was left in her care when his parents passed away. Jerry was in his late fifties and had some special needs. He brought a lot of laughter and joy to the unit.

He had his daily routines that included the care of his beloved monkey, named Monkey. Monkey was never far away. Monkey was Jerry's favorite thing in the whole world. He had pajamas to dress Monkey in at night, and pants and a vest for monkey to wear during the day.

He loved being up around the nurse's station, always greeting everyone with a loud "Hello!" I would draw pictures for him to color, and when he finished, would proudly display them.

Jerry had a cold for a couple of days and was not feeling very well. His family brought him a shiny Mylar 'Get Well' balloon with a monkey on it. Jerry treasured his Mylar balloon and proudly pointed it out to everyone who came into his room.

Jerry started having trouble breathing. The staff called 911 and got him ready to go to the emergency room. He was placed on a stretcher and wheeled down the hallway clutching his Monkey. The staff made sure the paramedics understood how important Monkey was to him and to please let the hospital staff know, as well.

This was Jerry's last trip to the hospital. He passed away from complications from pneumonia a few days later. As standard procedure, the staff closed off Jerry's room to keep it from being disturbed until the family could come and gather his belongings. In that room remained the Mylar monkey balloon.

On the day we received notice Jerry had crossed over, it was a little after midnight. The nurse for the west hall, Janice, and I were each in our charting rooms across the hall from each other. I turned around to talk to Janice and there was Jerry's Mylar balloon, floating in the air between us. The balloon remained there for about thirty minutes, until a CNA entered the nurse's station and was asked to return Jerry's balloon to his room.

At around 2:00 am, I was making rounds and noticed Jerry's balloon traveling down the hallway, heading in the direction of the nurses' station. I grabbed the ribbon tied to the balloon and walked it back to Jerry's room. The door was shut. I opened the door and placed the balloon in the far corner of the room, then shut the door and left.

I came across the CNA coming out of a room and asked her if she had returned Jerry's balloon when I had asked her to.

"Yes!" she said. "And then I shut the door afterwards."

She said the balloon had also made a trip into the sitting area where the staff would sit at night and watch television between rounds and client calls.

"I took it out of that room earlier and put it back in Jerry's room," the CNA said. Then she smiled. "Maybe it's Jerry."

We both smiled and agreed.

I started to make my morning rounds and medication pass when I saw Jerry's balloon in the hallway, slowly heading in my direction, which was also the direction of the nurses' station. When I came out of another member's room, I turned to my med cart and there was Jerry's balloon, brushing up against the handle.

"Hello, Jerry," I said, and left the balloon alone, wanting to see what it was going to do.

I returned to the nurses' station to do my charting. Within about an hour, the Mylar balloon was at the nurses' station again.

"It must be Jerry stopping by to visit," Janice joked. So we left it alone and the balloon stayed at the nurses' station the rest of the shift.

During the time that Jerry was alive and in the hospital, the balloon never left his room. It was anchored by a plastic disk. For it to have gotten back to the nurses' station two different times, it had to have traveled out of his room, making a left at the alcove, then a right to head down a straight sixty-plus-foot hallway. The balloon then would have to pass a cross-section of hallway and go through a half door, making a left into the nurses' station, traveling twenty feet, then through a doorway to the nurse charting area. No one could have brought it in there without Janice and me knowing, as an alarm would sound every time the half door was opened. The balloon came over the top of the half door by itself and the alarm never sounded.

The balloon was a way for Jerry to communicate by saying 'hello' and letting us know he was there.

Lynn

Every year, my mother would make the turkey, pumpkin pie, and yams for Thanksgiving dinner. After she crossed over, it was now my turn.

I had never made a turkey before, but I figured it could not be that hard. I read the label for defrosting the turkey and the temperature to cook it on. I took the turkey out of the freezer three days before to defrost in the refrigerator.

The morning of Thanksgiving, I started to prepare the turkey for roasting.

I placed the turkey breast up on the cooking rack and readied it to go into the oven.

"Do not forget the aluminum foil!" My mother's voice was loud, as if she was standing right next to me.

I thought I knew better and decided not to use the aluminum foil because I wanted a browned turkey like the ones on television.

Hours later, I learned why I needed the aluminum foil. Without the aluminum foil to evenly cook the turkey, the breasts were burned and the legs remained raw. Sadly, the Thanksgiving turkey was ruined and the family ended up eating hamburgers for that Thanksgiving dinner. I listened next time.

Five years after having my daughter, I was pregnant with a second child, a son. One afternoon, I distinctly remember being in my kitchen doing the dishes. I went to place a dish into the dishwasher, when I observed the spirit of a little girl standing there with her hands behind her back, leaning against the lower kitchen cabinets. The sweet-faced girl had medium brown hair and green eyes. Her face resembled mine. Her hair was shoulder-length in banana curls parted on the side with a Barrett. She appeared to be about 3 years old.

Somehow, I knew the little girl was going to be one of my children, even though I was pregnant with a boy.

I had several more visitations from the little girl. She appeared exactly same each time. Once my son was born, however, the little girl spirit did not appear anymore.

After giving birth to my son, I found out I needed to have a hysterectomy. Since my son was apparently my last pregnancy, I assumed the little girl might have been the soul of the current pregnancy waiting to come in as a boy instead.

I got good news and found that I did not need a hysterectomy, after all. Nine years later, I became pregnant at age forty-five and gave birth to a healthy baby girl at age forty-six. My daughter resembled me a lot.

One day, when my youngest daughter had turned three, she was standing in the bathroom with me, with her hands behind her back while leaning against the lower cabinet.

I had a déjà vu moment.

My youngest daughter looked the exact same as the little apparition girl, only without the banana curls. I realized the little girl I had seen while pregnant with my son had been another one of my other children who had stopped in for a visit prior to being born.

Gina

Gina was sitting in her father's hospital room. He was in and out of consciousness after a massive stroke. He wasn't doing so well. The doctor even recommended calling the priest for last rites.

The shift nurse entered the room to check his intravenous fluids. A short time after, a second nurse came in. She introduced herself as Samantha.

Gina reflected that her best friend in high school was also named Samantha, so it would not be a hard name for her to remember.

Samantha was very attractive, with high cheek bones and dark hair.

"Are you Indian?" Gina asked.

"I'm part Native American," Samantha said.

Gina felt love radiating from the woman. It humbled Gina to be in Samantha's presence. In that moment, Gina had a profound feeling that everything was going to be okay with her dad.

Samantha was very attentive to Gina's father. She also took time to answer Gina's questions and reassured her that everything was going to be fine. Gina was impressed with the time taken and the kindness of this woman.

The next day, Gina arrived at the hospital. As she turned the corner on the way to her father's room, she could hear his voice. He was chuckling.

When Gina walked entered his room, her father was sitting up with the respiratory therapist, cracking jokes and practicing with the incentive spirometer. Gina had gone home the night before thinking her dad would not make it through the night, yet here he was.

Still taken back by the kindness of Samantha, Gina wanted to write the administration a letter telling them about the wonderful care her father received from her.

Gina asked the respiratory therapist if Samantha was going to be working that day.

"We don't have any nurses named Samantha here," the therapist responded.

"I'm sure she said her name was Samantha," Gina said. "Perhaps I am saying the name wrong."

Gina described Samantha's appearance.

"We don't have any nurses named Samantha at all," the therapist said. "And the only two that are Native American are not nurses, and they don't match your description. One of those is a man. You may want to ask at the desk just in case they hired someone new."

Gina did just that and found the same answer: no one by that name or description worked there.

The doctor entered Gina's father's room and said to Gina's father, "We are planning to discharge you tomorrow."

Gina was thrilled yet surprised. The doctor told Gina's dad that he was a miracle, and he could not explain the sudden change in his health.

"I was visited by an angel yesterday," Gina's dad replied, "and she told me it was not my time, and I was going to be okay."

The doctor smiled and said, "It's good to have friends in high places."

He left the room.

Gina's father looked at Gina and started to tell her the same thing about the angel who healed him.

"It was a gorgeous Indian-looking woman with long dark hair," he said.

"Was she a nurse named Samantha?" Gina asked.

"No," her father said, "she was an angel sent to heal me."

He described the angel. Gina was certain it was Samantha. She had been in the presence of an angel of mercy.

Her father went on to live twenty-five more years, passing at the age of ninety-seven.

Paul

Paul was a little boy, about age five, in an abusive environment. Both of his parents were on drugs and Paul's father beat his mother regularly.

One day, Paul was in his bedroom when he overheard his mother screaming for help. He entered the room where she was and saw his father was holding a gun to her head.

Paul ran to the phone in the kitchen and called 911. He then ran with the phone and hid behind the living room chair, scared for his life and his mother's.

"An angel came and sat with me the whole time," Paul recalled.

Paul called him Jesus, and said Jesus sat with him, held him tight, and comforted him.

Once the police arrived, Paul said Jesus told him to go to the police and not to worry; everything was going to turn out okay.

Paul asked for Jesus to come with him, and he responded, "I will protect you."

Paul ran out the door to the police outside. His father was arrested and so was his mother.

Paul was unaware at his age how badly he had been neglected by his parents. He was placed in foster care with a loving family who ended up adopting him.

Chapter 8

What Happens After We Cross Over?

The spirit has left the body for the final time and has agreed to cross over. Their wounds are healed, and disease gone. They are no longer in pain. They are greeted by loved ones who coax and assist them out of their body, and from the third into the fifth dimension.

One may hear children speaking of a rainbow bridge, and someone waiting there for them, before passing away. They are welcomed home with a joyous, grand reception.

After the homecoming, at least one spiritual being of higher ranking guides the soul to a field covered in breathtaking beauty that is not describable with human words, where the soul is greeted by their deceased pets. And in the case of people who are more comfortable with animals than people, this can also be the other way around.

They are also able to attend their funeral or be present with loved ones at that time, if they want to. Remember, they can be in six different places simultaneously.

They are able to see other parts of the earthly planet that perhaps they had wanted to see while on earth but didn't get to. They are given time to rest and acclimate to their surroundings and renewed abilities that their physical body hindered, such as traveling by thought.

Once the reintroduction is finished, they begin their life review. The life review plays out in front of them like a movie in a cinema. They are not judged other than by themselves. They are able to feel every pain, every joy, and every shortcoming they caused. They are put in the other person's shoes and are able to see the rippling effects of their actions, both good and not good – every single act of kindness and unkindness.

They also review hurts and unfairness in their life, and the reasons for which they occurred. For example, say someone had a parent who had an addiction or an absent parent. They are shown what happened in that parent's life to cause the addiction or lack of good parenting. Their story is viewed from a place of compassion and not resentment. The departed are also shown the agreement they made with the parent before they came into the lifetime. They will see that the reason for it was for them to learn. They chose to have the outcome they did.

This all may be hard to believe, especially when you hear of a child being murdered. However, that child's soul may be thousands of years older than the adults on earth. They know death could occur early prior to coming in, and have volunteered to hopefully help the perpetrator make a better decision next time. It can also be the case that the situation is Karmic, meaning perhaps the child was the abusive parent once and is now the helpless child being abused.

Being an outsider looking in does not make difficult situations easier to tolerate. It does make an impression, though, and could influence people to a new awareness and influence them to take new more appropriate actions in their own lives. Everything is connected and happens for a reason.

The departed are also reminded of the agreement they had of what they needed to meet Karmically and had agreed to do in their lifetime. From the life review, the departed makes an outline of tasks still needing to be completed or redone. They also assess where they made new Karma or repeated old Karmic actions.

They are then taken to a place called the Akashic records. The Akashic records, or Akash, appear as an elongated room similar to that of a very ornate library, with information stored along the walls as high as the eye can see. The walls are covered with glistening gold shelves of light tablets filled with every word spoken and every breath taken in a lifetime. There are spaces both covered and uncovered. The ones uncovered are the opportunities taken. The covered are missed opportunities.

The departed one is shown the missed opportunities, as well as the outcome if they had taken the opportunity. The light tablets hold one's past lifetimes, most recent lifetime, and the future. They hold every thought, emotion, intention, action, or lack of actions, opportunities taken and missed opportunities. The records hold a recorded journey of one's soul, not only in the most recent lifetime, but through infinity.

In more modern times, the Akashic record is referenced as the Book of Life. It is mentioned in the Old Testament, in Exodus, as a record of one life that one is judged by. One should keep in mind that the Bible has been rewritten over a hundred times, with many books left out and changed to accommodate the writer's point of view. Some things in the Bible were changed over time based on different opinions of what would be better for the greater good, claiming it made the Bible easier to read and understand. The passage in Exodus detailing the record of everyone's life is accurate; however, the judgement comes from oneself.

Self-judgement is a better method, if you think about it. To be told what one did wrong is shameful, but often not totally owned. When one is their own judge, they are in full understanding and ownership of their actions.

These records can also be viewed when embodied on earth. Most people don't even know they exist, but it is not difficult to view them. They are in the energetic astral realm and can be a great source of information. There are restrictions, as some information may not be available for viewing due to timing. Some information given too soon could affect an outcome before its time. One can obtain not only information on their past, present, and future, but also of other paths. Perhaps one might want to look up the soul path of another. The records are considered to be where truths are held and made known.

There are many books written on the Akashic records and how to access them. In my experience, it is usually done through meditation.

Once the viewing is completed, one creates an outline of all they still needed to accomplish and are placed back in school. The buildings that hold the life review area, Akashic records, and school are near each other. Each building is more glorious than the next. It is hard to explain the appearance with earthly words. The buildings are seamless and smooth. The corners are softened by a slight rounding. The walls appear to be energetic within, as does the atmosphere. The atmosphere emits light from within itself.

Everything is in harmony with the sources in and around it, pulsating life in its purest form.

There is a flower there that my mother explained to me. The flower is called an Angel's Harp. The center is white with coral edges and its petals look similar to white shimmering feathers. It chimes the most beautiful melodious sound that only the connected observer can hear, and the sound that emits from its loving light energy is one of the most beautiful sounds she has ever heard. She said all things are alive there, and when something is focused on, the energies pulsating through it are felt by the admirer. It gently envelopes the observer and becomes one with them. The flowers feel you and you feel the life running through them, from roots to leaves to petals.

The vibrant colors are so magnificent. There are colors that are exclusively on the other side. There is no way to describe those colors. One would need an additional color wheel that we do not have here on earth. They are exquisite.

The homes on the other side are also seamless with rounded corners. The erected walls and buildings are all one piece.

The tall walls themselves are luminously translucent and opalescent in appearance. The roof covering is of the same material but more transparent. Night never occurs and there are no storms.

The school buildings do not have windows. They do not need them. The light emits from inside the opalescent walls, and at any point the wall can be looked through, from the inside out. They have desk-like tables with benches similar to ours on earth.

Souls are schooled in goals that they were not able to accomplish while on earth. They are often placed to oversee loved ones still on earth or with another person similar to who they were in life to help the embodied soul stay on track. Once schooled, they are sent back into a body to finish what they started, sometimes with the family group they left behind, or a paralleling one. This could be on earth or another planet similar to earth, in a different galaxy, of which there are many.

When one finishes their schooling, the heavens become like an airport with terminals, sending people off to their destinations. Everyone has a home to return to after each lifetime, if they chose to. However, there are a few special cases.

Serial Killers

In some very special cases, where a lot of traumas have been committed and endured, a soul can be cocooned after their life review and left in a resting state. Some, such as Hitler and serial killers, are cocooned after their life review, until rehabilitation can occur. If they cannot be rehabilitated, they are reabsorbed into the energy field in the universe and can end up in lower levels. Many times, they chose not to cross over and remain in the unpleasant fourth dimension.

Chapter 9

Spirituality and Religion

There are similarities and differences between religion and spirituality, yet they are not one in the same. The connection with God or a higher power and how long the concept has been around are two of the things they have in common. God has many names in each, yet they all mean the same thing. Spirituality recognizes this. Religion does not.

There are many names for God: Jesus, Jehovah, Allah, Yahweh, Adonai, Elohim, Lord, Holy Father and hundreds more. Spirituality encompasses them all by often referencing a higher power. Some religions embrace multiple heavenly deities, and so does spirituality. Other religions claim to worship one God, "the only God," since in their Bible it states that God is a jealous god.

Let's think about this. Since jealousy is a human emotion, and is regarded in the tenth commandment as something one must not do to be more godlike, then how can the statement about God being jealous be true? If it were, he would have to be a human, and also violate his own commandments.

Spirituality tends to unite people with commonality and loving acceptance. They accept every religion and love their neighbors. Most religions – especially Christianity – separate. They are willing to allow followers of other religious denominations to come and worship at their churches; however, the followers of the church rarely set foot in a church or synagogue of another faith unless it is to attend a wedding or other non-religious meeting.

Spirituality does not require a building to attend. Their temple is within one's heart and mind, though they do enjoy gathering with others.

In spirituality, people with gifts of the mind are accepted. In many religions, they are not. The words "clairvoyant," "mystic," or "psychic" can, even in this day, get one sent to the mental ward. People who are seeing dead people (called "hallucinations" by the medical field) and hearing voices (schizophrenia) are institutionalized or heavily medicated.

Following is a story I shared in my second book, *Omnipresent: What Happened Next*:

Amanda

I had gone back to school to further my degree in nursing. I had to do various clinical rotations paralleling the class I was enrolled in at the time. I was enrolled in a psychiatric nursing rotation. The class visited many of the institutions that treated mental illness and addiction.

One day, during this clinical, I met with my teacher and five other classmates for assignment of a patient to follow. The teacher explained to us that the area we were currently standing in was the intake unit, and to stay together and not communicate with the clients, as some may be combative.

As we stood together near the nurses' station, waiting for the instructor to return and assign us our person for the day, a young woman in her early twenties approached.

She looked at our group, then looked at me, and said, "Will you pray over me?"

I didn't respond, as I was told not to by my instructor. I looked around me, hoping she was talking to one of the other nurses near me, but she wasn't.

"Will you pray over me?" the young woman said to me louder, pointing at me. "You can help me, I know you can!"

Just then, the instructor came back over to our group.

"Do not say anything or make any eye contact!" She then moved us to another room.

My instructor asked for two volunteers to stay back in the high-risk "in-take" unit, and I volunteered along with another nurse. We were asked to sign papers that the facility would not be held responsible if we were harmed by a patient. We were not assigned set patients that day, but were there to observe. The other nurse and I were not sure what we were supposed to be doing, so we decided to sit down at a table in the common area and observe.

The young woman who wanted to be prayed over saw us and came over to ask if she could sit with us. We invited her to sit down. She seemed to be medicated heavily, as her words were kind of drawn out and slow.

"My name is Amanda," she said, and started to tell her story about why she was there.

"I hear twenty-five different voices that talk to me all the time," Amanda said. "Some of the voices hurt me."

She talked about one that was extremely frightening to her that had a large claw. She said that the claw scratched her everywhere, including the inside of her vagina.

"No one believes me," she said. "They say that I'm clawing myself."

While Amanda sat with us telling her story, I observed marks all over her, even in areas that would be difficult for her to reach. There were scratch marks on her face, arms, hands, back, shoulders, and even coming out of her ear. Amanda was wearing a tank top with spaghetti straps, and shorts with flip flops, so the marks were easy to see. Amanda talked about how she would wake up with more scratches and how the fresh ones burned like fire.

As I looked at her "scratches," I recognized them for what they really were – "claw marks," demonic ones. Demonic scratches look more like a single-clawed cat scratch. They are thin and bleed when inflicted deep enough. I have witnessed someone getting one in my presence. Human nail scratches are thicker and usually appear in multiples such as three paralleling each other.

Amanda went on to tell her story about how she was molested by the minister in her church when she was ten. When she told her parents, because of their religion, Amanda was accused of causing the rape to happen. It became her fault her father beat her and she was made to apologize to the perpetrator.

The raping continued for three years. Amanda was too afraid to say anything about it again. She prayed to God daily to please help her understand what action she was doing to cause the rape to continue. She felt the rape was her punishment for being bad, yet she wasn't doing anything bad.

"I wanted to die," she said. "I considered suicide."

Finally, her parents got divorced and she moved away with her mother, who no longer wanted to be affiliated with the church. Her mother remarried when she was fourteen and her stepfather raped her. When she told her mother, her mother didn't believe her.

Amanda became promiscuous and got into drugs at sixteen. Her mother kicked her out.

"I had nowhere to go and met up with the wrong group of people," she said. "They introduced me into Satan worship, which also meant a place to sleep and take a shower."

She was a part of that for four years. She knew it was something she did not feel right about doing, yet she felt loved, and at the time it seemed more acceptable than going to a church and being repeatedly raped then beaten for it at home.

This is also when she started to hear the voices talking to her.

She changed the subject.

"A nurse recently prayed over me," she said, "and it helped make the voices stop. I feel if you prayed over me, too, it would help even more."

The student nurse that I was on the unit with volunteered to pray.

Just then, Amanda's nurse facility came over to remind Amanda of her appointment with the in-house psychiatrist. Amanda stood up and started to walk towards the nurse.

As Amanda stood up from the table and turned her back to us to walk away, I could clearly see what looked like two clear plastic pillowcase-sized etherical sacks, one over each shoulder. They were filled with misshapen heads of various shapes and sizes. As I looked closer, I could see the faces on each, all clustered together like grapes.

My first thought was, "She's not kidding; she really is hearing twenty-five voices. I can see the attachments on her back. If this poor girl had them taken off, perhaps, she would not hear anymore voices."

I am not saying that all mental illness is demonic or attachments. However, I do believe that some of it is possession and attachments.

I knew that removing the attachments would be a huge job; much more that I could handle by myself. I also knew from my own experience that when dealing with demons, sometimes the activity gets worse before better, especially if you don't get them off all at once.

I returned to the unit after my lunch and found the young women. I told her that I believed that she was hearing twenty-five voices, that I could see the attachments on her back, and that when she got out of the facility, to see a Catholic or Episcopalian priest.

"In the meantime," I told her, "understand that those voices are from an external source. Do not to listen to them and do not accept what they are saying as your thoughts. Tell the voices 'NO!' and only listen to your own voice from within."

She again asked me to pray for her and I told her that I had been praying for her since I saw with my own eyes what she was up against on a spiritual level.

"Most importantly," I said, "you also need to pray."

"The attacks get worse when I do," she responded.

I suggested that she pray silently, since demons and lost souls cannot read your mind and can only go by what you are outwardly doing or saying.

While talking to Amanda, I looked at the way the demon clusters were attached. The attachment looked like a C-shaped horn that attached underneath her arm in the pit/axillary area and at the very top of her shoulder.

I felt compelled to stick my fingers under each horn and lift up. So I did.

I was surprised at how easily they came off and clung together. A few fell off and I stomped the ones that didn't roll away into the ground.

Amanda said it felt like hair being pulled off of her back when I lifted the attachments off.

"They can reattach," I told her, as I could see some clustered near her bed area. "However, it won't be as many. But please pray for protection and seek help like I told you to."

She was thankful and agreed.

"Also," I added, "if you mention anything about what just happened, you won't be believed and will be kept in longer. Your goal is to get out and get spiritual help."

After this happened, I started noticing in the facilities I was assigned to that most of the patients hearing voices had similar attachments. I knew their diagnosis was schizophrenia even before they would tell me. A lot of the addicts had archon-type attachments, as well.

I am not saying mental illness does not exist. I agree that people who see pink elephants climbing up the walls need help. I also think having a spiritualist and a priest on the admissions team at these facilities would make their census lower and less people on medication.

About a year later, I was shopping in a Walmart. I saw two young women standing at the opposite end of the aisle looking at me and talking. At first, I checked to see if I had something stuck to my shoe. When I didn't, I thought perhaps they were fans of my books and had recognized me.

Then I overheard one of the women say to the other, "I know it's her! I am going to go and say something to her."

The young attractive woman walked over and said, "Hello, are you Lynn?"

I looked at her. Her face was somewhat familiar, yet I could not place her.

"Yes," I responded.

"I'm Amanda," she said. She explained that I had helped her in the facility and she had found a priest willing to help her after she told him what I had said.

"He helped me," she said.

Now I recognized her, but she looked so different. She had lost weight and lightened her hair. She looked great!

She told me that she was in school to become a dental hygienist and was doing very well. I told her how thrilled and proud I was. She hugged me and thanked me.

"I'm off all of my psych medications except for a low dose of Ativan as needed for anxiety," she said.

I never saw her again after leaving the store that day. But I will never forget her, and still to this day, I pray for her.

A spiritual person would have recognized Amanda's issue for what it was and helped her. A religious person would see it as a psychosis and think she's mentally ill.

One may want to keep in mind that things of this nature may have been written about previously in the Bible. However, the Bible has been rewritten so many times, omitting over thirty-five books in the original documents, and the verbiage rewritten according to the writer's opinion and discretion. For instance, with the King James Version of the Bible, the sacred text has been altered repeatedly over the last two thousand years. No first edition exists. What we have are copies, the first of which were made hundreds of years ago after the biblical events took place. Also, the first Bibles were handwritten, and not by professionals. This led to omissions, errors, and most of all, changes. Some believe there were no changes. However, when the King James Version was written by King James I of England, it became the version that many Christians of today base their beliefs on.

During the translation of this version of the Bible, King James gave specific instructions to his translators regarding the content of the Bible he commissioned. He was specific about what sources could and could not be used.

The fifteen books of the Apocrypha were removed by King James I around 1769. This included the exclusion of a fascinating book, Wisdom of Solomon. The Apocrypha were not placed in the King James Version because it was believed they did not serve to validate any point of Christianity. The Apocrypha were, however, used by the Catholics.

I find it concerning that a religion can pick and choose which parts of God's word they choose to follow. It makes one wonder where religion would be today if they all followed all of the books originally written. It is more likely there would be one universal religion.

Traditional religions do not want to upset the status quo. They teach people in their congregations to shun anything different from the interpretation their Bible uses. They enforce their credibility by the modified Bible they have chosen to follow.

I distinctly remember a conversation between two of my coworkers who were of the same Christian faith. Their churches were on the same street, and they argued over which church was the chosen one.

Traditional religion manipulates followers with fear, because of the church's own need to feed off of the followers' money. They rely on the followers' money to exist. No followers, no money! No money, no church! Religion is a huge money-making business. Too bad they do not have stocks that one could invest in. It would be a great investment with constant gains.

I wish an original copy of the Dead Sea Scrolls was readily available to all for purchase. I believe that if one is going to follow something with heart and soul, it would be wiser to follow all of it, not bits and pieces of it. I feel that a lot about creation, dinosaurs, and extraterrestrials would be cleared up if we had the entire sacred book.

Religion and spirituality were intended. The problem with religion is the imperfect human souls whom we put our trust into to teach us and that we follow. Many times they do not walk their talk.

I met a minister on a dating site when I was single. After conversing back and forth for a period of time, we decided to meet up. We went out to dinner. The minister told me about his most recent girlfriend and how they liked watching pornography together. He told me that if things became serious with us in a sexual way, I could never attend his church.

He noticed I had rings on my toes and said it was sexy.

"You're not really minister wife material," he said, "but I'd like to see you again."

I evaded a response by shoving food into my mouth.

I was going to enjoy my dinner and finish it quickly. This guy was a scab.

He invited me back to his place for a drink. I declined.

He walked with me to my car, trying to change my mind. I was appalled.

"How can you stand up in front of your church and preach about adultery, yet be willing to have sex with me without being married?" I asked.

His reply was even more shocking.

"Well, I am a man, too," he said.

I was floored.

"You are a minister," I said. "You have to walk your talk twenty-four-seven. It's not like finishing your shift and clocking out and leaving, and the rest of the day getting to do as you please."

I'm okay with every religion or faith as long as it does not involve ritualistic killings, sexual acts with people under eighteen or who have not consented, or animals. As long as there is no harm to anyone or anything, I respect other's choices and don't judge. I make it a rule to talk very little about politics or religion. The subjects tend to divide families.

Some earthly religions teach that when a person sees a spirit, even if it is comforting and familiar, such as a loved one, that instead they are demons and to shun them. I hope that, regardless of your religious faith or beliefs, you know that your loved ones do want to visit you sometimes, and that it's okay. Welcome them and be comforted by them.

Chapter 10

Our Thoughts

On a scientific level, thoughts are the basis of our beliefs and triggers to our emotions. A thought is what initiates our response, both inwardly and outwardly. Our thoughts are influenced by our beliefs. Our beliefs are formed from what we experience and learn. Some beliefs develop over time and others are quick lessons.

Thought patterns can become ingrained without us even being aware of it. We also have certain thoughts habitually. Things can instantly come to mind automatically, with no effort. Therefore, the way one thinks is very important to their mental and physical health.

One area that is often overlooked when it comes to thought is how it affects us spiritually and how it affects our future outcomes. When we cross over, all of the communication is through thought. Therefore, our thoughts on the other side manifest into outward communication and travel. They also manifest desires; the thought of eating chocolate ice cream creates the sensation and flavor of it. Thought manifests everything one wants to experience. If you think of a person, you go to them. If you want to see a country that you were unable to visit in your embodied lifetime, you think of it and go instantaneously. Through our minds, we propel forward into the future or take ourselves back to a specific time or event in our past. On the other side, everyone knows what each other are thinking because it's right out front for all to see. Our thoughts are energy sent out into the atmosphere that then returns to us through manifestation.

While embodied on earth, taking responsibility for our thoughts is also very important, perhaps even more so. The reason is because, on the other side, the daily life hardships are gone. No worry is ever necessary due to having an all-knowing and all-seeing mind, one that can see all of the outcomes of every situation and action, while understanding its purpose. One also doesn't have to miss another because they can be present with anyone whenever they want.

On earth, our thoughts manifest here, too, but in a different way. The thought energy is released into the atmosphere, the same as it is on the other side. However, the manifestation is different. When thoughts are spoken, it makes the meaning of the thought even more intense. It's like sending the thought into the atmosphere twice. When one worries or obsesses over it, the thought is sent out as a message hundreds of times into the atmosphere. And, like prayers, those are heard and answered.

Unfortunately, joking, sarcasm, and worry of "what if's," "should have's," and "maybe's," and fear of many possible outcomes, will manifest just that. If not in the present it, will manifest in one's future, in one form or another.

When thoughts enter the atmosphere, they go into the universe. Since the thought is not directed to a specific heavenly being, it is returned as fulfilling a desire, wish or request. That's right! You will manifest more of the drama you are complaining about or loving, positive outcomes you are thinking about. It's your choice.

What compounds this even more in the earthly realm is that we so many responsibilities and activities of daily living to attend to; bills to pay, perhaps children or aging parents or pets to care for, getting to work on time, appointments, illness and car issues. We don't really have time to pay attention to all of our thoughts. Therefore, our thoughts run rampant.

Try paying attention for just ten minutes to every thought you have and see how many times a negative one occurs. Give yourself a mark for every time you have one:

- Worry
- Jealousy
- Negative thoughts towards another or oneself
- Obsession
- Panic
- Unworthiness
- Haughtiness
- Fear
- Emptiness

- Frustration
- Helplessness
- Sadness
- Failure
- Resentment
- Loneliness
- Guilt
- Inadequacy
- Anger
- Blame
- Negative assumption
- Elongated grief (beyond a year)
- Obscenities
- Depression
- Taking offense
- Thinking of physical pain, disease or illness
- Boredom
- Overwhelmed
- Discomfort
- Doubt

- Nervousness
- Negative intentions
- Cravings for drugs and/or alcohol
- Lack of something
- Desperation
- Feeling unloved, disrespected, or unheard
- Despair

Our thoughts manifest our outcomes in situations, disease in our bodies, and bring other negative or positive acts and thoughts to us from others. The more we focus on the negative, the more we set ourselves up for difficulty in life.

Even if you think of something then change your mind and do something else, it's all floating out there, preceding you; even words and thoughts in jest. "I'm going to kill….," "I hate….," etc. Even though you may not mean it, you are still responsible for the thought.

I am repeating this because it is important. The universe does not decipher between what one really means or not, it does not understand joking or sarcasm, it does not differentiate between a positive and negative thought or second guessing. It takes you at your word/thought and returns to each person what they put out.

Oftentimes we inadvertently cause manifestations in our lives we don't want or like. The manifestations are even stronger when "I am," "I can't," "I never," "I always," "I don't" are put in front of the other words.

For example, the person who says, "I never win anything!" will continue to lose. The person who says, "Dogs don't like me!" Dogs will continue to growl at or bite them. The women who say "Men always cheat on me!" will continue to attract men who will continue to manifest this for her. The person who complains that no one ever comes around to visit them, will manifest people not visiting them.

It is so important to retrain one's brain on the art of thinking more positively and manifesting wonderful things for oneself. It can be harder to do than one thinks. Most people don't even realize how many negative or neutrally unhelpful thoughts they have within an hour because it has become such a habit.

One way to start is to simply tell one's mind, "NO!" and force it to change the content to something more positive. This can be done in dreams also. The brain has become so used to the negative way of thinking. It is more comfortable and will resist. It's like a child testing the boundaries to see if they still exist. Be firm.

Have some things in mind ahead of time to change your thoughts. Most things can be rethought and stated in a way that brings positive returns. For instance, the person who has a visitor and complains the whole time about how no one ever comes to visit them could perhaps change their thoughts and words to, "I love seeing you and getting to catch up. I look forward to our visits."

Allowing this new way of thinking, with practice, it will become second nature. A smile goes a long way, too.

The brain will continue to try to do what it is most comfortable doing until it recognizes the new patterns of thought as routine.

One can change their thoughts of "lacking" to those of "abundance." Do it! Even if you only have ten cents to your name, envision yourself with millions. Stop yourself when you are fretting over the unpaid bills and see them as being easily paid. This action will either make a future of lacking and hardship or abundance. See yourself as you are in that moment as having all of your needs met, plus some extra. Then be thankful when the way opens for you to cover your expenses. It may not come in cash. It may come as resources that you have to reach out for or opportunities. Giving gratitude goes along way. Sense of entitlement does not.

Television, Video Games, Reading Material and Movies

What you fill your brain with is also not differentiated between when it comes to your thoughts and what one is visualizing. The visual stimulation records the same way. It evokes feelings, both positive and negative. For instance, during a scene in a movie where the favorite actor's foot is stuck on a train track and the train is coming near makes every one's heart rate go up. Their throat becomes drier and breathing either shallower, like holding one's breath, or faster. Even though you have not premeditated the train incident, it still affected you enough to make your heart rate go up, which means your brain has reacted to it first. The fear went out into the universe.

The mind does not differentiate between real and unreal when there is drama in it. You may have real life drama, or you may have watched a soap opera and are worried about the husband finding out that the married actress is pregnant with her boss's baby. So it is equally important what you stimulate your brain with. Violence is never good. Even though you know it's not real, your brain doesn't and still sends the thoughts out. Once the thought is out, it can't be taken back. It can, however, be counteracted by new thinking.

Nothingness

Have you ever wondered why some people can feel, see, and hear the presence of departed souls, but others cannot, even if the deceased loved one is standing right next to an unsuspecting person? For those who want to advance the ability to connect with both loved ones on the other side and higher beings for guidance, consistent meditation practices can amplify and enable that.

Everyone is born with the ability to see and hear spirit. Some have been shut down due to not being nurtured or being denied. Our early home environment is where the nurturing or shut down starts. People through the decades have learned to be afraid of their abilities. Even as things have evolved to more enlightenment, still most people don't believe in "ghosts" or don't want to talk about them.

Training the mind to be silent and in a state of nothingness opens the receptors for communication with the other side. This is where meditation comes into play. Once one reconnects with the other side, communication can flow freely, even when one is not meditating.

Meditation is not a time when you sit quietly and think about things. If this happens, it means your mind is still not open and is controlling your thoughts. Messages from the other side cannot come through if one's mind is not quiet and open. It gets easier to do the more often you do it.

Meditation is also great for relaxation, and thinking more positively can be a great benefit to one's health. It reduces stress and anxiety.

Chapter 11

Food for Thought

When souls cross over after relearning the way to do things on the other side, and one soul approaches the other, they are able to peer into one another, seeing each other's lives before and the progression of the soul itself.

When souls who have crossed over travel back and forth to visit loved ones or a place on the earthly plane, they travel in orbs or enter through portals. The portals are openings in the veils that separate each dimension.

It is said there are twelve upper dimensions/planes and seven lower dimensions. The dimensions exist separately at the same time and occupy the same space. Each has their own energetic frequency, color, and vibration. Frequency refers to the state of awakening and consciousness. Vibration refers to an energetic source or light within us that we resonate with and connects us to others who have the same vibration. That is how light workers and anchors find each other.

A human can be physically on the third dimension and raise or decrease their vibration through their conscious decisions and actions. In other words, a physically grounded third dimension person can also be of the fifth dimension because their consciousness is there. In this third reality, it is often a hard task to evolve from its hold. It takes a lot of determination, enlightenment and constant actions that are greatly rewarded.

Humans can have energetic and astral access to the first five dimensions from the third dimension. Earth is a third dimensional space. Unfortunately, many humans are comfortable remaining at the third level and prefer to stay in their limited awareness. They don't advance, and sometimes this even lowers their vibration. It's all about choice in a realm where there is no discrimination and equal opportunity for all. The twelfth dimension is God's private space.

On our current plane, Earth, we are embodied to function with our surroundings. On other planes, human-type bodies may or may not be needed.

Some humans have evolved spiritually and are able to be in two or more planes, third and fifth, simultaneously. This is called ascension. Everyone has the ability to attain ascension while on earth and embodied. It is what a lot of people here on earth seek but never find.

Every soul seeks this ascension spiritually, whether they know it or not. It is a subtle hunger, a craving for the ambrosia. This is ignored by many and often dulled out by addictive behaviors. Addictive behaviors are third dimension and lower.

Souls on the other side communicate with us through telepathy by transferring thought directly. Often the voices go ignored. How many times have you been in a grocery store and had an overwhelming urge to get an item? Then you don't purchase it, only to return home and find that you were out of it. How many times have you had an inner voice warn you not to do something and you did it anyway, only to regret it? That vision that pops in one's head of accidentally cutting their finger right before it happens, or dropping an item right before it's dropped and broken. One may find themselves thinking, *I knew that was going to happen* or *I should have listened.*

When one listens to their inner voice, they call it listening to their intuition. The intuition is actually helpful suggestions from the other side.

Whether they are present or not, it seems as though our loved one is talking directly to us or standing right there. They can visit in dreams, too. Remember to ask that you are able to remember the dream when awakened.

However, there are parts of the fourth dimension that have started to mesh together with the third (earth), allowing more and more unembodied souls to linger and enter. Unembodied souls are dead people who have not crossed over and others from the lower levels.

The fourth dimension, where lost souls live, is also an energetic freeway for many other beings, including demons. Demons enter when invited by invitation. The invitation can be calling them in by misuse of Ouija boards, or automatic writing by someone who fails to close the portal behind them. The passing of souls leave portals open and people with lack of experience sometimes carelessly dabble in the darkness. (Then they call someone like me to come to their home and get what they let in out, because it won't leave on its own.)

Our loved ones and guides on the other side will assist us when called upon. However, because of their higher frequency out of body, they are not able to approach or assist one until situations are calmer. Their increased vibration can unintentionally exacerbate situations, both negative and positive. In other words, they watch with a careful eye from a distance so as not to increase the volatility of a situation.

In cases like this, they work around the periphery, sending other earthbound sources in, such as a dog to stay with a lost toddler in the woods, or a neighbor who overhears a commotion and calls the police, or even the shock of a mouse running over one's foot with perfect timing to distract them and prevent something more critical from happening. Whether one realizes it or not, that delay getting to work because you are stuck behind a school bus may very well be something that saves your life literally miles down the road.

Everything really does happen for a reason. It is all connected. Your loved ones on the other side can see the outcomes before it happens. Because of this, sometimes they do not intervene at all, especially when the outcome will be a good one, or a necessary negative one. Perhaps a negative outcome needs to happen to make one more aware and prevent something much worse from happening in the future. Or one simply needs to learn a lesson that will make one's life easier if not repeated. Lessons are there to guide us onto the path we are meant to be on. They help us get back on track when we go off.

Aliens

It's no secret that aliens really exist! We are just waiting for our government to finally admit it. There are many galaxies with solar systems with earthlike planets and humans similar to us created by our same creator. Many beings are more sophisticated and advanced, while others are behind.

Some are highly enlightened beings that work alongside angels in the fifth dimension, and who also come forward when one is transitioning to assist and welcome the spirit home. They are called "alien" because they are not from this earthly plane. Not all aliens appear green with big heads, and the ones who do aren't seen on the other side.

Aliens appear similar to the grandeur of angels, but without wings. They also communicate with telepathy and their light is bright. Most stars in the sky are light sources for other solar systems. It would be obtuse to assume we are the only living souls that exist. Depending on the galaxy and sector they come from, some can appear Homo sapien; others do not. Like any being, they are able to manifest things with thought.

Aliens are not always the big headed, small bodied creatures with enormous eyes that fly around in spaceships. That kind does exist, though, which has been verified by thousands of abductees worldwide. Most abductees don't even know one another, yet they share stories that are hair-raisingly similar.

A lot of controversy has been raised about how much the government actually knows, and the possibility of the government actually working with them but keeping this knowledge from the public. In this moment, I may not be able to prove this theory; however, it can't be disproved, either, by sceptics. There is more proof that they exist than that they don't.

At the time of one's crossing over, deceased loved ones come forward, angels come forward, and beings of great illumination and magnificent beauty also come forward. They are un-winged, very tall, and stand out in the crowd. These advanced cosmic beings are the last to leave the room with the newly deceased and walk along with the angels assisting.

Aliens such as the grays, which are the kind to fly around earth's realm in ships, are very different. These are the ones that abduct people and mutilate cows. These are also the ones who collect and mix human ovum and sperm with alien species, as well as other insects and animals, creating atrocities, and then dumping them off on earth to see how they fair. They are advanced and use portals to cloak themselves and remain stealthy.

I believe Big Foot, also known as Sasquatch, is one of those alien creations. Has anyone ever wondered how a very large, extremely smelly being such as Big Foot can become odorless and completely disappear when cornered? According to multiple sources, there have been tens of thousands of sightings in the states of Pennsylvania, Washington, and California alone. Big Foot has been photographed by people. They have an overwhelming methane smell that can be recognized from significant distances away. There is evidence of footprints, and yet in an instant, when cornered, Big Foot can disappear – smell, footprints, and all – when pursued by people trying to trap them.

Somehow Big Foot is advanced enough to use the same etheric veils and portals to cloak themselves and disappear that aliens use. I personally have seen, with my gift of second sight, aliens do this act more than once.

Marsha

On a Saturday night in March 2005, I was working a twelve-hour shift as a nurse in an upscale skilled unit of a long-term facility. I loved this job because I was able to build a rapport with the members and their families.

At around 10:00 pm, a member named Marsha at the end of the hall called for her nightly medication. I grabbed my newly charged blood pressure cuff and her medication and headed down the hallway to the last door on the left. Her door was open, so I hesitated.

"Knock, knock," I said, since my hands were full and I was unable to physically knock.

To my surprise, as I stood in the doorway of her room, she was not the only one there. Her room had no lights on. I could see Marsha with the light that illuminated from the hallway. I observed her lying on her side, facing the door, along with five other beings in the room.

The five beings stood opposite me on the other side of Marsha's bed. Her back was facing them. She smiled and greeted me, and invited me in.

Trying to make sense of what I was seeing, I set my things down on Marsha's table and prepared to check her blood pressure before giving her medication. Oddly, my blood pressure cuff ran out of battery before I could finish putting it on her wrist. I called out to a nursing assistant who was nearby in the hallway and asked her to bring me down a new cuff.

While waiting, I spoke with Marsha and watched the beings in her room. They were all methodically working on Marsha. They appeared to be pulling plugs and re-plugging them into a different part of Marsha's body. The motion was like that of an old-time switchboard operator. They did not stop even though I was there. They appeared to be working behind and through a veil. They ignored me.

I heard the nurse assistant coming down the hallway. I stepped back into the doorway and got the blood pressure cuff from her. I checked it and the battery was full.

As I came forward to the bedside, one of the beings came around to my side of Marsha's bed and walked right through me to continue its work. As the being went through me, I felt a brief static tingling and squeezing sensation.

"Excuse me," I said.

Marsha thought I was talking to her.

I went to apply the blood pressure cuff once again, and once again, the cuff's battery was dead.

Each being was about four feet tall. All five beings were about the same height and body build, and dressed in the same white or gray space-type suits. They stood upright and had humanoid bodies.

Their faces were covered with the same material as the suits they wore. It was as if they could see right through the material over their faces. The top of the head covering came to a point and laid back loosely, flopping to the back of their heads, creating a squared-off appearance from their front. Because of the material over their faces, I was unable to see features.

I walked out of the room to obtain a manual blood pressure cuff, thinking they might leave. But they were still busily working on Marsha when I reentered her room.

I do not think the aliens realized I could see them. I did not say anything about them to Marsha. I could only imagine how uncomfortable it would make her feel, me getting ready to medicate her while talking about seeing invisible things in her room.

I gave Marsha her medication and headed back down the hallway to the nurses' station.

I checked on her thirty minutes later to follow up on the effectiveness of her pain relief. When I entered the room, the beings were gone, and Marsha was still asleep on her side, facing the door.

I never saw the beings in any of the other twenty-three rooms.

I was assigned the same hallway every weekend for ten years. About six months after the first incident, I again went to give Marsha her nightly meds, and this time counted three alien-type entities in her room doing the same plugging in and unplug thing. This time, one of the beings was about a foot taller and slenderer than the other two, who were identical. They again wore the same uniform as before and appeared to be working through a transparent veil.

Two months later, I saw eight of the same identical beings in her room.

Marsha was on my hallway for two years before she died. I saw the beings a total of three times around Marsha in her room – in her room only; no one else's.

Once Marsha died, even though her room was assigned to new members over the next eight years that I worked in the same facility, never again did I see the alien beings.

Having the ability to peer into this alternate reality is known as interdimensional viewing or second sight. Interdimensional viewing is something we are all born with the ability to do and is not exclusive to humans. Often because of one's upbringing, this ability to see inter-dimensionally can be shut down at an early age.

In society, children who voice what they see inter-dimensionally are often told they are not seeing anything and that nothing is there, or that ghosts do not exist. Some may be told it is a deceased loved one or guardian angel watching over them. Others are disciplined by their family or church for having this ability. Even in this more modern day and age, where awareness is heightened, traditional religion does not support the possibility of this. They continue to shun it.

Children learn to deny interdimensional abilities to fit in with the norm. The longer the time they are disconnected from their ability, the less familiar they are with it. Most people end up becoming terrified of entities from other realms and avoid even talking about such things. But they do know deep down that such things exist, whether they admit it or not.

Zachary

I had gone with my oldest child to an appointment with a licensed counselor for help with her ADHD. As we sat in the waiting room, a little boy was brought out to his mother. The counselor informed the mother the entire visit had been done in the dark, and the boy had no issues with the darkness.

"Well, I don't understand why he will not sleep in his bedroom," I overheard the mother say, "and insists on sleeping in the living room on the couch."

As the counselor and the boy's mother continued to speak with each other, I looked at the boy. I noticed a great light that beamed from him, especially his forehead area. I recognized this as the child having developed second sight. J

My daughter leaned towards me and said into my ear, "That boy is psychic." I nodded my head in agreement.

While my daughter was with her counselor, I took a moment to speak to the boy's counselor.

"Could I share some information with you?" I asked.

It was a blessing that she was open minded, too. I told her what I had overheard in the waiting area and that I was not asking for information on the child.

"I simply wanted to tell you the boy is not afraid of the dark," I said. "He is afraid of what comes to him in the dark."

She nodded her head and I continued.

"I would be curious if someone had died at some point in the room that is now the boy's bedroom, or if the family has noticed any spirit activity in the home. If it is the case, perhaps suggesting he change to a different bedroom might help."

Two weeks later, while my daughter was in another appointment, the woman returned with the boy she called Zachary.

When Zachary was called back with the counselor, his mom said to the counselor, "You were right. We changed his bedroom, and he sleeps in it every night with no problems."

While her son was still in his appointment, the mother was on the phone with someone telling them how they had inherited the house from her husband's aunt and that she had died in the bedroom Zachary had been originally given.

"The bedroom change worked," she said. "Zachary hasn't asked to sleep on the couch in the living room since."

It is very important to empower children and to give them the skills not only to say "no" to strangers, but also to spirits who are frightening them or making them feel uncomfortable. Just because you cannot see them, doesn't mean they are not there. Pay attention to your own actions when your child approaches and informs you of their ghostly visit. This is something you may not have done before. Are you feeling a bit uneasy or getting chills? Do you linger to play with your child in the room in that moment, or do you high tail it out of there, finding something else to do in a different room? Teach your children a prayer or song of protection to sing out loud to make the daunting presence leave.

We are not only protecting ourselves from criminals at large; we also need to protect ourselves from the unseen spiritual warfare going on around us.

Chapter 12

From the Other Side

Some of these messages have been echoed throughout the chapters of this book. I want to put more focus individually on these messages and explain in more detail.

Spirits who have crossed over can make themselves clearly known to us here. They come and go as they please and are always with us. It helps that they can be so many places at one time. The meetings are always a pleasurable experience. Their visits are never intrusive, frightening, or weird. They often enter our dreams or leave evidence for the intended person to find.

Both souls who have crossed over and those who have not usually appear dressed. Those who have crossed over are seen in robes or the clothes they were placed in after death. The reason they appear dressed is because the majority of incarnated people on this earthly plane have been taught to shy away from public displays of nudity. Even if one is comfortable with being nude, our society has rules about that sort of thing. Plus, I can't think of many people who would want to meet up with their nude grandparents on the other side. It would be hard for most to look at them upon reuniting, let alone embrace them.

They can move things. They don't do it in front of you because they know that can be frightening for a person here. They do this to let the earthbound loved ones know that they made it to the other side and are okay. It will happen when you least expect. However, in some cases, maybe not right away.

Sometimes the visits after crossing over are subtle and can be overlooked or doubted. The spirit will wait for the perfect time.

I say "after crossing over" because lost souls can also show up. They show up in person and not in your dreams. Once a soul has crossed over, they can hear our spoken words and unspoken thoughts. An earthbound lost soul can only go by our spoken words and physical actions.

At any given time, we have multiple magnificent beings watching over each of us individually. We have guardian spirits; they are not all just angels. They can be our loved ones, and sometimes an assigned spirit who is there for their own learning and growth as well as ours. The assigned spirit can be a family member, or they may not be, and they interchange. Once a goal has been met, that spirt is replaced with another who also needs to do more work on themselves by helping the earthbound soul redirect and take a better path.

These spiritual suggestions are gentle nudges the embodied soul can choose to use or not. The spirit guide is learning by the benefits of the embodied soul's choice. The spirit guide is placed with a person who has similar issues to unresolved issues that they themselves had while earthbound.

Even if the person continues on a perilous path, the guiding spirit still learns, as they can see the similar mistakes they had also made in life from a different point of view. The spirit comes from a place of understanding and love. They are aware of the person's background and life goals. They are also aware of the possible outcomes ahead of time. For instance, in the case of an alcoholic; did the person stop drinking? The spirit cannot interfere or change the outcome. They can only guide the person with encouragement to meet their goals.

Our loved ones and guides on the other side patiently await a call for assistance by those on earth. They can be activated by our call. Keep in mind that if the embodied person calls during a time of great duress and emotional upheaval, it can negate the spirits' ability to come closer until things are more emotionally settled. As mentioned earlier, the higher frequency of spirits from the other side causes emotions to exacerbate, so anger becomes rage and happiness becomes elation. This is good for positive emotions, but not negative ones. Unfortunately, we have a tendency to call out for heavenly help when things are more negative than positive.

Spirits of our loved ones would love to be called on daily instead of when a mess has been made of things. Their assistance could have helped thwart a negative event by assisting one in making better choices. At the very least, one's reaction to a negative event could be improved to prevent the rippling effect of rage. Our loved ones on the other side know our triggers and can help one think in a calmer way when triggered. They never force or interfere. They wait to be asked for help.

Even a car hitting a tree can be a positive. I know it doesn't sound like it, but often things such as that that turn out to be troublesome in the beginning make us more aware, preventing something much worse later on. A person texting while driving may look up to see a deer running across the road directly in front of them and they swerve, hitting a tree. This occurrence gets one's full attention. It can make that person think twice about texting and driving, and could very well have saved them from an accident much worse minutes to hours down the road. They should be thankful neither they nor any of their loved ones were hurt.

It's the same concept with frustration over the older lady or new driver getting onto the Interstate slowly. They might very well have been placed in your path to slow you down those few seconds in order to prevent something tragic happening to you down the road. Be thankful. Send the person love, not obscenities. When you do, your life review you will be brought back to that very moment, and you will see the loving gesture the deer and the tree, or the old lady or new driver, did for you and how nicely or badly you acted. Their act could have been a lifesaving event. Many things happen for a reason.

Messages

The most important things are to love all and to keep one's thoughts and emotions harmonious. Then comes the understanding that one's departed loved ones are NOT gone; they coexist beside us, come when spoken to or called, and can communicate with us directly if our minds are open and ready to receive.

Marked changes in the world's vibration are becoming more noticeable as they continue to occur. Recognize earth as a living thing and love it, too. Love can be sent to anyone or anything though your heart space. Envision anyone or anything and while holding that thought. See love like echoing sonar ripples being sent directly from your heart to the designated source. Love is the only emotion that is real and the only vibration that can heal.

Make changes in yourself. Making personal changes for the better ripples outward and positively affects those around us. Some positives may not be seen, like having someone who is negative leave your life or loss of a job. One may not realize the benefit in the moment, yet will in future.

There is always a divine plan. Look upon the course of your years. It's not people who have taken your freedom; it's a limiting attitude and consciousness. Obstacles are not God's will. They are incidents that give our souls opportunity to raise its consciousness.

Nothing in the emotional world can affect you unless you choose to give it attention. Where you focus your attention is where your life energy goes. Where your energy flows, such as worry over problems, the more one is manifesting more problems in their future. Stop doing this!

Disconnection from the drama that surrounds us and reconnection with God, one's higher self, or the creator (all are the same), which knows your soul journey and true purpose, is essential more now than ever. Unconditional love and oneness are the only energies that permit all to be viewed free of judgement.

It is important to come to terms with any addictions prior to passing over, as addiction can prevent spirits from crossing over easily or at all unless the spirit is willing to leave the substance behind.

Religion

Every faith crosses over. There is no religion in heaven. Religion as it is known on earth is far from godliness. No religion teaches unconditional love, though Christians preach it, along with biblical quotes that they do not apply to themselves. They separate through denominations, including the non-denominational ones, which is a very misleading term. They criticize and judge those who attend other churches. Those who do not attend church at all or who are not Christian are sometimes referred to as "pagans." (Just so you know, "pagans" are also the creator's children and cross over, too.) It is NO person's place to judge anyone. Judgement is hatred!

Religion professes to teach love, and yet they teach fear of the spirit world that is all around us. Those spirits who are standing by to help guide us. Religion deceives, and mentally works through guilt in order to dominate and manipulate.

Church is one of the biggest financial institutions in the world. They have to judge and defame other religions in order to keep the money coming into their church. Our creator doesn't care about having money. If religion mirrored the God they profess to worship, then there would be no religion! It would not exist. Love would be spread across the planet and universe. No religion will take you into the heavenly dimension, because they do not and are not practicing unconditional love. You go to heaven anyway, with or without practicing religion, but not because of religion. You cross over because of your personal connection with our creator.

Just because someone goes to church does not mean they are practicing what they have learned there. Not even the leaders of the church are all practicing what they preach. They slip up and blame it on imperfection. Like having sex with children or cheating on their partner, and then excusing themselves because they are sure they will be forgiven on the upcoming Sunday. Everything they do, everything they think, every breath they take is recorded and never forgotten. Everything is recorded and they will face it again, as well as the rippling effect of their actions.

You don't need a religion to show you the way. You connect with heaven/the other side with your heart. No rules, no dogma, no religion, no tithing. Let go of beliefs and concepts that are leading you down the wrong path. Unconditional love to all is the only path. No exceptions. No excuses.

Unconditional love is your direct line to all of the heavenly beings. It is the way to true happiness.

Some people, depending on their religious beliefs, need more time to adjust and get acclimated to the surroundings on the other side, especially if they were conditioned by their religion to think that only their church would go to heaven.

When a person leaves the earthly realm, it is because it was their time to leave, regardless of the way the death occurred, with the exception of suicide. Get rid of the blame and guilt, wondering if you did enough, wondering what their future might have been like, and grieving that loss for the rest of your life. Whether it's an accident or purposely done by someone, know that the deceased lived out their time here on earth and completed their contract. Nothing could have stopped the death.

There is a little wiggle room (a few days) with the time of death on earth. That is because heaven's time is different than ours. As I mentioned before, their days are years long in comparison to ours. One's time of death/departure is set in heavenly time. Their minutes are equal to days here.

The Grocery store

I was on my way to my job and stopped in a grocery store to pick up something for my dinner. As I stood in line, a man in front of me was preaching and handing out religious pamphlets.

The man offered a pamphlet to me. I took it and said, "Thank you," not because I had any interest to be recruited into his religion, but because it was a kind gesture from a person with good intentions.

Then he offered one to a young lady behind me who dressed in all black.

She respectfully said, "No, thank you."

The man got a little louder and started to shame the woman for not accepting the pamphlet.

"I'm Wiccan," the woman explained calmly, and again said, "No, thank you" to his offer.

The man started raging and screaming at the woman. He called her all sorts of judgmental names and made threats of damnation. She stood there silently.

The manager had to intervene, as it was alarming to all of the customers in the store, who were now gathering to witness the commotion. The police were called.

Even as the man was walked out of the store, he loudly recited scripture, almost frothing at the mouth.

The young woman never said a word.

I asked her if she wanted me to walk with her to her car and she accepted.

As we walked into the parking lot, the man who had been calmed by the police officers started heckling the woman again, trying to shove past the police officers. One of the officers came forward and asked the woman if she wanted to press charges against the man.

"No," she said, "just detain him until I am way down the road."

The woman thanked me, got into her car, and left.

I looked down at my hand. I was still holding on to the pamphlet I received from the man in the store. It said right on the front, "What would Jesus do?" I had to chuckle to myself as I thought about which of the two customers, the man or the young woman, were acting more like Jesus in that moment.

Everyone is born with second sight that will either be nurtured or shut down. Second sight is the ability to see spirits. Many people are seeing spirits and do not realize that is what it is. Ever catch a glimpse of something out of the corner of your eye? And you would swear that you saw it, but then when you look directly at it, nothing appears to be there? That is a considerably basic form of second sight. It usually starts out as spirits seen in one's peripheral vision.

When going from the peripheral view to looking at it directly, the frequency shifts and it appears that nothing is there. One who is not experienced or open to using their second sight will see nothing, yet the vision one had in their peripherals is still there.

Both the frontal, direct view and peripheral view can be enhanced. This happens first by acknowledgement, then through meditation; silencing one's mind, withholding fear or anticipation, and prayer asking for assistance with the viewing. Sometimes acknowledging the realization of other dimensional beings is enough to increase one's ability.

Oftentimes a person will hear a frequency or fleeting ringing sound in one's ear. This is also a form of spirit communication. When a spirit is close but not right next to you, perhaps on the other side of the same room as you, the frequency change is heard in the left ear. If the frequency change is heard on the right side, the spirit is within reaching distance or right next to you. The spirit realm walks among us.

People who have the gift of second sight are often considered mentally and emotionally unstable by the legal and medical communities. There are lots of medical "disorders" and "terms" for it: hallucinations, delusions, and sometimes, schizophrenia. Their belief is labeled occult by traditional religion. There are, overall, lots of labels and judgements from fear-based people. The truth, though, is that we are all born with the ability.

Psychological studies have shown that children between newborn and age five do not have certain mental filters. They lack discernment, also known as common sense. Not having these filters in place, from a spiritual viewpoint, allows children, and also people nearing death, to have access to their spiritual family on the other side effortlessly.

The filters are built up (or not) by the way we are taught to perceive things.

These filters separate our earthly plane from the multiverse. The filters thicken as the child gets older, often slowing or decreasing the child's ability to see spirits and hear them.

When puberty begins, even those children with abilities that have been nurtured experience them temporarily lessening or stopping. They begin fully returning, sometimes even stronger, later, after puberty ends.

Often with children, this ability can be interfered with by others telling the child that "there is nothing there," "there are no such things as ghosts," etc., and they can be disciplined and accused of lying or told there is something wrong with them. They can be accused of being possessed or told they are going to hell. Sadly, they are taught to fear their natural abilities to connect with the other side and death.

Invisible friends are real, and are not guardian angels. When a child has an invisible friend, or speaks of seeing someone you cannot, it is always important as a parent to make sure the invisible friend is not making the child feel uncomfortable or asking them to do something they would get in trouble for. There are many kinds of spirits. Some are not always what they appear to be. These questions rule out something more malevolent, though most invisible friends are harmless.

The filters continuously thicken as a child approaches age five, which is when most children start to speak less often about their invisible friend.

Humans can maintain the ability of second sight from childhood or retrain their souls to do it. Embodied souls who elevate their frequencies through prayer and spiritual evolvement can travel inter-dimensionally during their dreams, meditations, and intended astral projections. Often they can communicate with loved ones and the entities they come across. They can receive guidance from glorious masters and teachers from the heavenly realm. This takes consistent work and dedication on the embodied soul's part to achieve.

Most people would see a spirit and respond with fear or discomfort. This fear is the main reason people cannot see their loved ones who have crossed over.

Aliens (Again)

There other types of aliens who are reptilian or insect-like. They do not enter dimensions past the fourth dimension; their vibration is not high enough to enter the fifth or above. They are able to manipulate the veils between the dimensions up into the fourth. They manipulate portals to move in and out of the earthly space.

They are the ones abducting earthly people for tests and mutilating livestock. They are mixing species through fusing semen and ovum from different species. They are in search of the essence of our souls, which is our light and spark given by our creator. They will never find it. Either you have it or you don't! They don't, and thus are also void of feelings such as love.

Chapter 13

End of Life Directives

Death is about living the way one wants to right up until they take their last breath. Death is a very real part of our life cycle. Death is not prejudiced. It happens to everyone.

Death does not set an appointment with you. Because of this, it is important for everyone to make their end-of-life directives known, and also empower another, whom they trust, with the ability to speak on one's behalf when they cannot speak for themselves. This will help to ensure their wishes are honored and reduce the burden on the remaining family. This is very important advice. You will be glad to have this knowledge when the time comes for you or a loved one. It is important for any age to know and can be done for free. You don't need an attorney.

When one does not make their end of life wishes known, loved ones often react based on their fear of loss or regret and avoid the discomfort of grieving. They do not have time to thoroughly consider what is best based on the dying person's current medical standing. They are emotionally stressed and unable think clearly.

For some, this can be a very uncertain time. They may worry that they have not done enough for the loved one. Or they may start grasping at straws, hoping that one more thing might change the situation for a better outcome. Watching a loved one dying can be one of the hardest things a person will ever go through.

Often because of this, the loved ones choose to have measures taken to sustain life that are more traumatic than helpful, and the result ends up being the same. A lot of times, when a terminal or transitioning soul has come to terms with their body, readying to cross over, they want to talk about death. They often do not have anyone to listen or ask questions. They do not want to place the burden on a distraught family, who is bargaining for more time and a miracle.

Sadly, these days, most doctors do not have time to sit down and answer all the questions and give support. Death and dying is a subject that is more often avoided. Most people do not feel comfortable talking about dying or death until they are forced to. Death can be profoundly sad for those being left behind. The finality of death often creates fear and anxiety in people and their loved ones.

One way to ensure that one's wishes are honored, not only about what happens after death, but also during the process of dying, is to have a healthcare power of attorney, also known as HCPOA.

Some people do not realize that an HCPOA is or can be separate from a power of attorney, or POA. The HCPOA is established so one has an advocate to express one's desires and wishes, such as treatment and comfort measures to be taken at the time they are needed. This is for when the designee is unable to speak for themselves and make their own medical decisions.

Oftentimes hearing anything with power of attorney in it can be intimidating. Many people think that it gives someone the power to pull the plug when the loved one is not ready or to sell their house out from under them. It is important to choose someone or several people one trusts and are trustworthy.

Often people never designate a HCPOA because they think that one actually needs an attorney to make it legal. They avoid doing it due to concerns of cost. You do not need an attorney, nor do you need a lot of money. There are "do it yourself" forms in places like Office Depot and online. A form such as a free "Five Wishes Form" that has been filled out and notarized by the person designating it is a legal binding document. It can be changed at any time with further notarization and is only activated when one is unable to speak for themselves.

I want to repeat this. The notarized form is nothing more than a piece of paper that sits there unless the designee is unable to speak for themselves. Even after it is filled out and notarized, if the designee is alert and oriented and still making good decisions on behalf of their life, the HCPOA document remains dormant. One's doctor's office should have a copy for if something ever happens, as well as for the designated person.

Putting the document in a safe or locking it away defeats the purpose. The document needs to be accessible when needed.

A good place to consider is inside your refrigerator. Yes, a refrigerator, not freezer. Place your document inside of an airtight waterproof plastic bag and tape it to the inside wall. According to the National Institute for Fire and Safety, what's inside of a refrigerator fares well in a fire. Refrigerators do not usually burn in house fires. Also, if there is a flood, your refrigerator might be floating down the road with you hanging on to it and your important papers safely inside. Not to mention that if criminals at are robbing your house, it would be a rare situation for them to be looking in your refrigerator.

Again, even if your doctor has a copy of your document, they still have to address all of one's health care needs to the designee unless it is determined that one cannot speak for themselves.

Another example is if one arrives to the emergency department unconscious, the HCPOA can make decisions for the designee on their behalf. If and when the designee become conscious, oriented, and able to speak for themselves, once again the HCPOA steps back and becomes dormant until needed again.

Another thing to be aware of is that just because a person brings their spouse, for instance, who is designated HCPOA with them for an outpatient procedure, and someone from the hospital admitting comes in with papers to be signed by the client, those papers should be addressed to the client only. If the client gives permission for their spouse to have access or sign on their behalf, then it is okay to allow the spouse access. However, it is always better for each adult individual to sign for themselves. One never knows for sure what the outcome of a hospital visit or illness will be. Often the person signing gets to pay the bill. I am not discouraging paying your bill. I am encouraging not to get stuck with someone else's bill and for the living person to protect their financial future, just in case the hospital visit takes a turn for the worst and your loved one passes away. Just because one is the HCPOA does not make them responsible for the bill. Being married or related does not, either, unless they sign to be responsible. Do not sign to be responsible for anyone's bill except your own or your child who is under age eighteen.

Janice

Janice, a good friend of mine, and her husband Jeremy, both in their late forties, went to the outpatient department at the local hospital. Jeremy was scheduled for lithotripsy to break up his large kidney stones. While getting undressed and into his gown, the young lady from admissions knocked. She had some papers for Jeremy to sign. Janice was on the phone with me at the time and asked me to hold on the line.

Since her husband was preparing for his procedure, she says, "I am his Health Care Power of Attorney, I can sign the papers."

I was still on the phone overhearing this conversation.

Without question, the admission clerk handed the forms to Janice. Janice signed the forms and handed them back to the admissions clerk.

Janice returned to our phone conversation. I asked Janice why she was signing the documents for Jeremy.

"Well, I'm his HCPOA," Janice said.

"No, you're not," I said. "On paper you are, however that paper means nothing unless Jeremy is incapacitated."

I continued to explain that not only did Jeremy walk into the outpatient unit himself, but I could hear him talking to the nurse in the background. He seemed alert and oriented and was answering questions appropriately. Janice confirmed that he was.

"So you are not supposed to be given those papers to sign," I told her. "Go back to the clerk and ask her to shred the signed papers and reissue them to Jeremy so that he can sign for himself."

That day, Jeremy had an allergic reaction with complications that caused him to spend ten days in the intensive care unit before passing away. The hospital bills, even after his insurance paid their part, were close to $30,000. Janice was devastated and grieving her loss. She was also adjusting to a single income on a two-income budget.

The bills started coming in for Jeremy. Janice was not able to pay them, and she became concerned that she could lose her home because of it. She went to an attorney. The attorney asked Janice if she signed anything at the hospital for Jeremy.

"No," she replied, "he signed his own papers for everything he had done."

The attorney told Janice that was fortunate, because Jeremy's bills would come for him at thirty, sixty, then ninety days, and then they would be turned over to collections.

"Jeremy's credit will be ruined if they are not paid," the attorney said. "However, Jeremy is dead."

He reassured her that since she did not sign anything, the bills would not be able to affect her credit, nor was she obligated to pay.

Again, I am not saying don't pay your hospital bill. If the outcome for Jeremy had been different and he had not passed away, he and Janice of course would have paid the bills off together. But since he died, Janice could not afford to pay them. It would have placed her in a long term financially devastating situation that could have been avoided. I can assure you Jeremy would not have wanted to leave her with that burden. I have seen similar situations like this happen over and over. Family members making payments for years on a deceased loved one's medical bills when they don't even have enough money to pay for their own life sustaining medication. Do not sign for someone else and do not allow anyone to sign for you. Other than your underage children, there should be very few reasons for you to sign for someone else. If a client themselves is alert and oriented but unable to physically sign for some reason and the HCPOA is asked to sign, say "I am not authorized" since the client is still able to speak for themselves and the hospital can have two witnesses (hospital employees) verify a verbal signature from the client.

The Five Wishes form is free. It is an excellent economical source and is legally binding once notarized. It is easy to fill out and, as its instructions walk one through the process, it explains how it works legally and how one can change the HCPOA if needed. It also gives ideas of some other choices a person can make that they may not have even considered. It even has an area to write a note to your loved ones. The Five Wishes pamphlet is free online with no strings attached and can be printed off. If a site is found that does have any strings attached, such as payment, you're on the wrong site.

You print off the form, fill it out on your own or with trustworthy persons, and have it notarized. The only cost incurred is for the ink and paper used to print it off and the notary. Another to note is having this document does not take away from current arrangements, such as a living will. It is a tool to complement any existing documents specifying end of life directives.

Several important notes to make here is that once death has occurred, all of the HCPOA and POA are null and void. It is important to designate people to handle your affairs after death, an executor (male and unisex) or executrices (female).

Another important thing, be sure if you have a joint checking account with your spouse/significant other, that it is worded your name "or" your spouse's/significant other's name. It should not be your name "and" your spouse's/significant other's name. In some states, the word "and" will close the account down, leaving no access to the account without legal intervention. It is also important that arrangements be made with your bank, if you are not sharing a checking account jointly, so that after your death, designated family members have access to the money in your account without having to obtain an attorney.

In this day of technology, once a person passes away, the social security office is made aware; and with that, everything affiliated with one's social security number can be shut down. The process that once took days is now addressed within a few hours.

Most people prepare for their retirement. They prepare for life events such as graduations, college, and purchase of a home or car. They prepare for smaller things what meal they will eat next. Usually, death preparations are put last or until absolutely necessary. Often this lack of preparation leaves families to deal with all the details during a time when they need to grieve. This also leaves them vulnerable to paying more than they would have if they had had time to price shop. The same caliber of arrangements can be planned but for less money, unless you can afford it. Funerals are for the living, not the dead.

Once a person dies, if preparations have not been made, there is an extremely short time for the family to make decisions of what funeral home to use. Most facilities expect the body to be removed by a funeral home within four hours of death.

Death preparations are similar to preparing an important life thesis, in the sense that the plan for preparations can be changed and added to or subtracted from at will until all the details are exactly the way one wants them. Making end of life wishes known to loved ones does not mean a person has to run down to the nearest funeral home and pay for their funeral. It can be as simple as making known whether they want to be cremated or buried.

When making the decision of whether to be cremated or buried, it is important for the person choosing one or the other to consider if their family they are leaving behind will be left with a debt that will affect them adversely long term. This factor is equally important to the departing loved one's personal preference about either. The family being left behind needs to be left in good condition financially. If there are concerns of this, then prepayment is a great option to protect your family's finances when the loved one has passed away and for the loved one to have their wishes met.

Often people are unaware of the cost of a funeral until someone passes and they have to pay for it. A simple small obituary itself can cost hundreds of dollars. Perhaps a good idea would be to allow one's family to choose what they need for their own personal closure, and then based on that, what they can actually afford without causing hardship.

Not making one's end of life directives known could leave the family at the mercy of the funeral home. Once the body is at a funeral home, one must trust that they are being charged fairly, as a funeral home is a business. I can promise you, once your loved one has left their physical body, they care more for their loved ones still here than their arrangements, and do not want to burden their family financially.

Another thing to consider is if a person is in their nineties, would you want an end of life service to be something smaller and close-knitted, with mostly family, that can be recorded and shared with others, or a big all-out funeral that not everyone would be able to attend? Many times, at older ages, a lot of our deceased loved one's friends have already passed away ahead of them or are in facilities and would not be able to attend.

The thing about natural vs. sudden death is that with a terminal diagnosis or natural decline to death, one has time to get things in order if they choose to. The transitioning soul has some time to accomplish things to make life easier for their loved ones after they have died. They can check off some items on their bucket list and tell people how much they appreciate and love them, and vice versa, or they can tell loved ones where the money is buried. They can prepare birthday cards and Christmas cards to be given after they have left this plane.

Perhaps the declining loved one might want a celebration of life before or after they crossover, instead of a funeral. If a celebration of life is held before the person crosses over, then they themselves can participate in it. For someone terminal, it is a gathering, usually with food and their favorite music. Often the person has pictures of their life and digital videos. People get to tell them directly how they feel about them and say goodbye.

A celebration of life can also be done after death instead of a funeral. Perhaps a person wishes to donate their body to science or be encapsulated to be revived in future decades.

Perhaps because of their religious beliefs, they do not wish to be embalmed, or they may want to be buried within twenty-four hours. With some religious faiths, if they have had an amputation, they need to bury with all their body parts.

Wayne was ninety-three years old when he crossed over and all of his friends had already crossed over before him. So he asked his family to have a small beachside gathering with his favorite dish – potato salad – and to play Pink Floyd's "Off the Wall." He wanted his ashes sprinkled both in the water and near the shoreline where he had walked almost daily for the last sixty years of his life.

Buried or cremated? Sometimes going straight to the facility that cremates is less expensive than a funeral home. Often crematories offer full service, just like the funeral home does, but much more economically, if the loved ones are financially struggling. Even if one is not financially struggling, why pay an extra $2000+ if one does not have to? There are also cremation societies that can cremate a loved one often for less than $1000. Funerals are more for the living than the deceased.

Often people hear the outcome of their terminal diagnosis, or that death is imminent at any time, and they die mentally in that moment. They do not make the most out of those precious remaining days. They choose to lie in bed and give up while they wait for death to happen. This is really a time to get things in order.

People who have come back from sudden near-death experiences speak of their instant thoughts after death. Many have stated that once the shock of being dead wears off, they find themselves thinking about all of the things they did not finish or say. They regret not being able to complete what they feel is necessary. And when they are allowed to return, they make sure to do all of those things they remembered wishing they had done.

If you have a spouse or loved ones, it is wise to write down a detailed list of where things are or who has them.

- Make a list of investments, with whom the account is with and the account numbers, the amount of the investment, and who to contact with a phone number.

- Write down where the safety deposit box is and where to find the key. Notify the bank that upon your death, the designated person has the authority to open the box. Make a list of what is in the box.

- Where income tax papers are from the previous seven years.

- Insurance policies, account numbers, and who to contact with phone number.

- Who holds the loan on one's car or where the title is.

- Write down to the phone numbers to notify social security and the retirement pension, if applicable.

- Where the mortgage is held, the account numbers and contacts, or whereabouts of the deed.

- The last time the oil was changed, or service was done on the car.

- Any warrantees, with whom, and for how long does the warrantee last.

- Where DNR, POA, will, and HCPOA papers are. Make sure your will is up to date and beneficiaries are who you want them to be. (Wouldn't want your ex taking your kids or new spouse's inheritance. You don't need an attorney for a will, either; get a form from Office Depot, print one offline or write it out on a piece of paper and have it notarized. Be sure to give a copy to someone you trust and not a party in the will.)

- Write down who your electric, water, internet, garbage pickup and cable company is, with along with account numbers and when payment is due each month.

- Write down who your car, boat, motorcycle, life, cancer policy, AFLAC and home insurance is with and contact number with accounts numbers.

- If one has a pet, when their shots are due, the name and phone number of the veterinarian, and groomer.

- Items to be returned and to whom, as well as items to be collected and from whom.

- Write down anyone who owes one money and how much, along with the payment arrangements and contact information.

- Any upcoming appointments and with whom so they can be canceled.

- Any investment property someone may not know about.

- Homeowners' fees, how much and to whom it is paid and when it is due.

- Medical Insurance policies, account numbers and with whom, with a contact person and phone number.

- Time share information and contact.

- Lawn service, cleaning service, dry cleaner where family clothes may be.

- Age of roof of one's home and company who did roof.

- Checking and savings account numbers

- Passwords to computer, credit accounts, email, and Facebook/social media

- Hidden keys, to the lawnmower, shed, car, boat, tractor, mailbox, and motorcycle

- Hidden money (especially if one had hidden money and jewelry in clothes pockets, to check shoes and clothes before giving away or donation.)

- Your wishes for your pets and who to take them.

- Custody of children if both parents are deceased.

- Trusts, who has and contact information, and what are the terms.

- Safe and lock combinations

- List the valuables in one's home. What your family might think is just an ugly painting may turn out to be an original Renoir or Picasso worth millions.

There is a lot to do to make the loved ones being left behinds' lives easier. Have repairs made that have been put off on the car and house, or paint and replace.

One has time to make a pact with the declining loved one. They can agree on a calling card, so to speak, that their loved one's spirit will leave when they come to visit the embodied soul. It can a scent, hair, feather, etc. These comfort loved ones here on earth.

My mother, Phyllis, and I made every minute count before she died. Life is not the gift we all believe it to be. Where we come from and return to is. However, every second of what we do here on earth matters on both sides.

About the Author

Lynn Monet, world-renowned author of the highly rated *Omnipresent* series, is a paranormal consultant and lecturer. She has been a nurse for over thirty years and spent seventeen of those years working in geriatrics and end of life care. She has a degree in biological science and is on the Board of Directors for Health and Recovery magazine, to be released in 2023. She is an empath with the ability to see frequencies most cannot. Her ability allows her to observe the transitioning of souls from the physical realm into the spiritual realm at the time of their last breath. She peers into the other side and observes the joyous inner workings and grand reception for loved ones.

Edited by Ivy Sweet, ivymae.sweet@yahoo.com

Printed in Great Britain
by Amazon